Innovation and Entrepreneurship

Strategies and Processes for Success in Tourism

Edited by
Prof. Dr. Klaus Weiermair
Prof. Dr. Peter Keller
Prof. Dr. Harald Pechlaner
Prof. Dr. Frank M. Go

With contributions by
Werner Bernet, Valérie Brive,
Prof. Eileen Fischer, Dr. Elisabeth Fischer,
Prof. Dr. William Gartner, Prof. Dr. Frank M. Go,
Grzegorz Golembski, Ronald Israels,
Prof. Dr. Peter Keller, Dr. Christopher Kronenberg,
Dr. Paul Lynch, Samir Markarem,
Prof. Alison Morrison, Marcin Olszewski,
Prof. Paola Paniccia, Maria Razumova,
Christopher Reuter, Bartolomé Deyá Tortella,
Luiz Gonzaga Godoi Trigo, Marco Valeri,
Prof. Dr. Francois Vellas, Prof. Dr. Klaus Weiermair,
Dr. Anita Zehrer

ERICH SCHMIDT VERLAG

Bibliographic information published by Die Deutsche Nationalbibliothek
Die Deutsche Nationalbibliothek lists this publication
in the Deutsche Nationalbibliografie;
detailed bibliographic data is available in the Internet
at http://dnb.d-nb.de.

For further information concerning this title please follow this link:
ESV.info/978 3 503 11611 9

ISBN 978 3 503 11611 9

This paper fulfills the requirements of the
Frankfurter Forderungen of Die Deutsche Bibliothek
and the Gesellschaft für das Buch concerning the paper permanence
and meets the tight regulations of American National Standard
Ansi/Niso Z 39.48-1992 as well as ISO 9706

Printing and Binding: Danuvia, Neuburg

Preface

The idea for this published collection of cases of innovative entrepreneurship came from two of the editing authors of this volume who attended the 10th Enter conference in Helsinki (Technology on the Move).

As usual with conferences of this kind the emphasis of this conference had been on introducing, employing or distributing new technology in tourism dealing in the main with technical-analytical issues. But what about the most important motivating force behind the third industrial revolution now also embracing tourism e.g. the innovative entrepreneur? The latter though extremely important for innovation had been missing in the discussion. And thus the idea was born to investigate and report on the most innovative firms and/or entrepreneurs in tourism to be found across a number of European and non European countries. The central idea was to pick only those innovative entrepreneurs in tourism who had changed business practices in the industry in an almost revolutionary fashion; in short we wanted to find true "Schumpeterian" entrepreneurs across 13 countries where we had the possibility of accessing firms. To avoid biases in the selection of the innovators a two stage selection process involving both industry associations, public tourism boards and academics was chosen yielding an industry and academic consensus as to who in those jurisdiction was the leading innovator in the field of tourism broadly defined. The case histories, it was hoped, should help identify similarities and/or differences in the underlying determinants and currents of innovation and innovation processes in the tourism industry.

When looking below at the success stories of innovation in tourism in 13 different jurisdictions we find in line also with some of the general interpretations of entrepreneurship and innovation in tourism provided by K. Weiermair and F. Go in this book a dominance of the following 5 success factors:

1. Existence of appropriate entrepreneurs and entrepreneurship
2. A vision for needed paradigmatic shifts or changed business concepts
3. Translating the vision into appropriate management and organisation development processes creating "intrapreneurship" and continuous learning and growth
4. The choice for the right place and time to introduce new products or processes in tourism
5. Supportive governmental or public policies and/or programmes

Entrepreneurship played a crucial role in all 13 cases reported although it did so in different ways. Whilst in the Austrian, Canadian, Finnish, French, German and Italian case an individual entrepreneur had been at the center as the prime motivation force showing vision assuming risks and shaping institutional and market arrangements, "Strategic Partnerships or Collective Entrepreneurship" was more responsible to create effective business plans, strategic vision and/or new products commensurate with innovations in the case of the Brazilian, Dutch, Polish, Scottish, Swiss and U.S. case.

Every innovative entrepreneur or group of entrepreneurs needs a vision about a new product, a new process, a new form of marketing, new markets or new forms of organisation.

A vision of course does not always imply or lead to revolutionizing the nature of tourism business practices, in some cases innovation may simply involve product line or market extensions or involve creative imitation of business practices in other firms or markets (see the Brazilian, German and Polish case studies). In all of the other cases we can observe rather large changes of business concepts based on visions of anticipated changes in tourism demand creating in the main a new type of experience in tourism. E.g. the very successful introduction of cultural goods & services (Swarovski, Austria) new adventure experiences (G.A.P, Canada and Touring Cars, Finland) health products and services (RP Care in Holland and the Salt mine Bochnia in Poland) novel food experiences (Ayrshire Food Network, Scotland) and medieval destination/hotel experience (Sextantio Albergo Diffuso, Italy). Alternatively three entrepreneurs have created entirely new ways to organize tourism with respect to financing tourism (Swiss Travel Bank managing tourism destinations, Transmontagne in France) and marketing tourism (Carlson Destination Marketing, USA). All cases attest to the strong customer and market driven aspect of innovation as the key to success.

Although not as transparent and articulated in all cases was the third innovation success element of translating vision into appropriate management programmes and policies. In the main it involved such aspects as putting in place continuous learning, quality improvement and/or R & D programmes (Swarovski, Austria; Transmontagne, France; Joska Kristall, Germany and the Green Card Balearic Islands, Spain) or the management of alliances and/or partnership which was of importance as success factors in all of the other cases.

As is also explained subsequently in the next chapter, time and place play a key role in determining the likely success of innovations in tourism. Thus most of the innovations reported in the 13 case studies take either place at the beginning or towards the consolidation phase of the destination life cycle and all are positioned close to important sourcing markets.

Finally the last factor which in our case studies has helped contribute to the success of innovation are benign or supportive governmental programmes and/or policies towards firms innovative efforts. In one extreme case the government itself was the innovator (the Green Card programme in Spain) whilst in the remaining other 12 case studies governments supported innovation either through outright private public partnership (the Polish case) or through different forms of funding or financial aids available at different levels of government. Given the shifting interests of today's governments away from subsidizing ailing firms and industries towards supporting innovative firms and future industries tourism firms in some European jurisdictions have thus been able to reduce the high risk and cost of innovation thus facilitating major product or process innovations.

The present volume documents these 13 case studies of innovative entrepreneurship alluded to above and at the same time provision is made at the beginning and at the end of these reported cases to provide some additional insights with respect to the external setting of innovations in tourism (e.g. at the beginning with K. Weiermair Tourism development and Entrepreneurship) and at the end with the firm's internal innovation process and its managerial implications (F. Go: An Interpretation of Case Studies on Entrepreneurship and Innovation in Tourism).

While it was probably impossible to account for all types, determinants and success factors of innovation in tourism across all jurisdictions and across time it is hoped that this volume will nevertheless provide both theoretical but above all practical insights into successful innovative entrepreneurship in tourism.

Klaus Weiermair   Innsbruck, Januar 2010

Contents

PETER KELLER

Introduction

The role of entrepreneurship in tourism was for a long time ignored or neglected. The literature in this field is rather poor. It is the merit of Prof. Klaus Weiermair to have founded the IEN network which analysis entrepreneurship as a driver of innovation in tourism. Prof. Weiermair is in the tradition of Schumpeter who defined the entrepreneur an actor who tries to improve his economic position by innovating. The idea for a publication "Entrepreneurship and Innovation in Tourism" was born at a Seminar of the OECD Tourism Committee on the role of innovation in tourism in June 2006 in Rome (Italy). Authors from twelve different countries analyze entrepreneurship in cases where innovation took place. The goal of the publication is not to present just "best practices" but to give an insight on the importance of entrepreneurship under different circumstances and framework condition and also different stages of product and process innovations. One of the co-authors, Mag. Christopher Kronenberg, put carefully together the cases. In conclusion of this publication, the results from the cases are analyzed and summarized by Prof. Frank Go from the Erasmus University of Rotterdam (Netherlands)

1 The Often Neglected Role of Pioneers as Early Tourism Entrepreneurs

There are only few publications about entrepreneurship and tourism. This is somewhat surprising in a sector where the actual structures had been largely initiated and put on the market by pioneers. These personalities had the qualities of entrepreneurs. They founded palace hotels and hotel chains, leisure parks and holiday clubs, cable cars and cruise ships, tour operating and reservation systems and a lot of other important elements of the actual tourism system.

The important role pioneering entrepreneurs in the field of tourism was always linked to the organizational structure of their firms. The tourism related industries are essentially small and medium sized enterprises (SME's) where the owner is often also the manager. The same personality develops *new business ideas and takes the responsibility to implement the ideas in the market*. This double role links inspiration and creativity with transpiration and endeavor. It brings together ideas from outside the firm with experiences from inside the firm. These are good prerequisites for innovative processes. It is the reason why tourism related SME's are still bedrocks for innovation in tourism.

2   Entrepreneurs as Main Independent Innovators in Tourism

Entrepreneurship is one of the most important resources for firms in market economies. Entrepreneurs are looking for the most profitable business. They know their environment and enrich this knowledge with the experience of their business. They anticipate new social trends for which they develop new products, processes and forms of organisation.

The tourism structures of today *are above all the result of entrepreneurs who acted in the sense of Schumpeter by trying to improve their position through innovation, taking risks and who, with total commitment and at great personal risk, changed the way people do business*. It is to such people that we owe today's tourism structure with outstanding luxury hotels, leisure parks, hotel chains and "low cost carriers".

Tourism is the playground of *independent innovators*. Innovation passes in tourism through the entrepreneur. It is in this sector not a strategic activity of the management as it is in the industry where investments in innovation are a routine. There are no division for research and development (R&D) in the field of tourism related industries and destinations.

3   The Role of Entrepreneurs in the Innovation Process

Entrepreneurs play an important role in the innovation process of tourism. They implement their vision and business idea by using the experiences inside and outside their enterprise. They adapt major tourism relevant basic and applied innovations from other sectors step by step to the needs of their own firm.

The role of entrepreneurship could be analyzed by taking cases from all tourism related industries or destinations. The example of jet aviation explains quite well the interdependence between the inputs from the entrepreneur and his firm and the inputs from the business environment and structural change. Jets made travelling fast and cheap. This basic transport innovation led to important changes in the field of international tourism. Tourism entrepreneurs used the new possibilities for opening new markets in an innovative way such as the charter flights or package tourism.

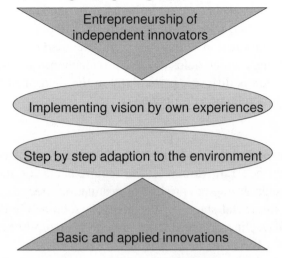

Figure 1: Entrepreneurship in the innovation process of in tourism

4 Innovative and Replicative Entrepreneurship

For Baumol innovation is the marriage of new knowledge, embodied in an invention, with the successful introduction of that invention into marketplace. It is only through *"innovative entrepreneurship"* that means commercial activities that embody some new product or service, or method of production or delivery – that societies advance their technological frontiers and thus their standards of living (Baumol et al. 2008). Baumol sees the opposite to innovative entrepreneurship in what he calls *"replicative entrepreneurship"* which means producing or selling goods or services already available through other sources. Replicative entrepreneurs have an important function but are not a primary source of growth.

The differentiation in innovative and replicative entrepreneurship is important. In the field of innovation it is not the size of firm which matters. *Entrepreneurship must not be confused with small business.* The majority of SME's is led by entrepreneurs who are not innovative. But independent innovators start often with smaller firms. Larger or more established firms take over, refine and mass produce innovations from entrepreneurs.

Hilton and Mariott in the USA for example, started as family hotels and developed then the most successful standardised hotel chains mainly to meet the needs of business travellers. An attack on the monopolies of traditional national and network carriers was first launched by two pilots from Southwest Airlines and has led to an explosion in low cost airlines in all continents.

Innovative entrepreneurs are often imitated by the competitors which refine the innovation and take advantage of them without having the costs of preparation and introduction of innovation into the market. *Creative imitation* is a business strategy which helps to mass produce innovations. It is the main way that innovation is diffused, particularly in the field of SME's which operate under the umbrella of a destination.

5 Entrepreneurship and Lifecycles of Products and Destinations

Entrepreneurship is a rare resource. The requirements for successful entrepreneurship change during the product or destination lifecycle. Entrepreneurship is needed in crucial stages of the lifecycle such as the discovery stage and the stage of decline. In these cases entrepreneurship is needed (*see contribution of Klaus Weirmair and Christopher Kronenberg*).

Entrepreneurship *competencies and skills may change during the lifecycle of a product*. In the case of the cable car industry which is a leader of tourism development in mountain areas, entrepreneurship of promoters who know the tourism resources of a given territory is needed during the initial stage of development. In the boom stage with its environmental problems entrepreneurs with competencies in negotiation are required. In the stages of maturity or decline, entrepreneurship with focus on marketing and financial competencies is needed.

6 Entrepreneurship in a Mature Sector

Entrepreneurship is a complex resource. It is therefore important to analyze cases for explaining the real importance of entrepreneurship. The focus of this publication is to show *the richness and the variety of entrepreneurship* in the field of tourism.

In a mature sector such as tourism, there are still a lot of success stories. But they are mainly the result of replicative entrepreneurship. They do not have an impact on future growth. They cannot solve structural problems of mature tourism. The cases the authors of this study deal with are often not spectacular. *But they focus on really new and innovative solutions for old problems*.

In the stage of maturity, *new entrepreneurial strategies must be developed and implemented for making "old tourism" new and more performing* (Weiermair, 2008). In such a situation, creating new attractions and developing new products is necessary for rejuvenating the existing supply. Such a strategy needs new forms of collaborative relationships rather than independent lifestyle approaches currently employed by many SME's. Tourism related firms have to produce in a more efficient way. They also have to look for new solutions for financing upgrading investments in tourism equipment and installations (Figure 2).

- Create new attractions by using the existing endogenous growth potential
- Develop new products for rejuvenating existing supply
- Produce in a more efficient and sustainable way
- Look for collaborative relationship within and outside the sector
- Overcome adverse framework condition

Figure 2: Entrepreneurial strategies for rejuvenating mature tourism

7   The Highlights of the Cases

The cases fit with the entrepreneurial strategies for mature tourism related industries and destinations. They cover the whole producing and selling tourism system with its markets, resources and framework conditions (Figure 3).

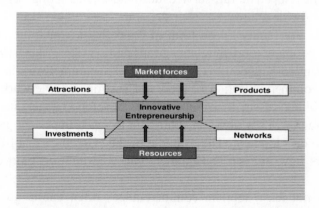

Figure 3: Entrepreneurship and innovation in the tourism growth

Attractions are the basic resources of tourism. In mature tourism economies, natural and cultural attractions are well-known. New manmade attractions are necessary for attracting visitors. The *Swarovski Crystal World* (Austria), the *Joska Kristall* Exhibition (Germany) and the *Spas of the Salt Mine Bochnia*

(Poland) are such manmade attractions. They function like some sort of a dream factory which imagine, plan, promote and put on stage emotional experiences.

Investments for providing targeted goods and services are a necessity for those who want to visit the attractions. Investments in hardware are expensive and need adequate financing solutions. *Swiss travel bank REKA (Switzerland)* finances its activities as the leader in the field of rented and serviced apartments for the family segment from selling travel checks to its customer which are subsidized by employers and retail firms. *Transmontagne* (France) invests with new business ideas into the rejuvenation of medium sized mountain resorts in the Alps which have the double problem of weakening winter sport tourism and still insufficiently occupied summer tourism facilities. *Touring Cars Finland LTD* is one of Europe's leading camper rental-company which imports motor homes, sell them to private people who give them free for renting to third parties. This financial system allows them fast growth and diversification of risks.

Products are bundles of services. Their development is part of the core business of tourism. The *G.A.P. Adventures (Canada)* develops a local niche activity into standardized and internationalized product. The most important Dutch leisure park enterprise *"Roompot"* (Netherlands) offers to its customer holidays combined with targeted health care. Specific bundles of services are also offered by *"Carlson Destination Marketing Services CDMS* (USA)"*. This firms developed a full-service destination marketing service agency which is worldwide unique.

Networks are finally a lose form of cooperation which are necessary to develop and promote tourism related goods and services. The *"Airshire Food Network"* (United-Kingdom) is an example of such a network in the field of supply and commercialization of food and gastronomy. Networks can overcome the problem of small size and help to develop endogenous growth potential of a region. They also can contribute to reach important goals such as a sustainable development. The example of the "Green card" of the Balearic Island shows how tourism stakeholders can contribute to more sustainable tourism.

Last but not least, tourism commercializes often public goods such as landscapes or cultural heritage or security or safety. Therefore the **States framework conditions** are crucial for tourism business. Strong leadership is often asked for developing firms under difficult framework conditions as the Brazilian case shows.

8 Entrepreneurship as a Common Ground

The common ground of all the cases is *innovative entrepreneurship* which creates growth, employment and income in tourism. There are many descriptions of what can be considered as an entrepreneurial personality. The authors speak with respect and even admiration about the entrepreneurs whose work they have analyzed. Innovative entrepreneurs are described in the Polish case as that who "introduce totally irregular changes, upset the existing balances, smash old habits and ultimately creates new structures".

Entrepreneurship is need for managing all the variables of the tourism system. It can be defined as *a vision and business ideas which are put into practice by leadership.* Such visions, business models and leading qualities are almost omnipresent in the cases presented. The founder of customized and standardizes adventures, the investor who rejuvenates forgotten Alpine resorts or the leader of the food and gastronomy network are indeed real entrepreneurs. Entrepreneurship is neither restricted to the size or the form of organization of the enterprise or the organization. The interaction between shareholder, managers and all the other stakeholders can also enhance it as the example of the "Swiss Travel Bank REKA" or "Roompot" make clear.

References

Baumol, W.J. (2002), The Free Market Innovation Machine, Princeton University Press.

Baumol, W.J., Litan, R.E., Schramm, C.J. (2007), Good capitalism, bad capitalism and the economics of growth and prosperity, Yale University Press.

Go, F. (2005), Co-creative tourists: An idea whose time has come, in: AIEST, Innovation in Tourism, Creating Customer Value, Vol. 47, St. Gallen.

Keller, P. (2008), New Paradigm for Tourism Policy, in: Tourism in OECD Countries 2008 Trends and Policies, Paris.

Keller, P., Bieger, T. (Ed.), Innovation in Tourism, Creating Customer Value, Publication of the AIEST, Vol. 47, St. Gallen.

OECD (2006), Innovation and Growth in Tourism, Paris.

Weirmair, K. (2008), On the Changing Structure, Conduct and Performance of the Tourism Industry: From "Old" to the "New" Tourism, in: Change Management in Tourism, Berlin.

Weirmair, K. (2006), Product improvement or innovation: what is the key success in tourism, in: OECD, Innovation and Growth in Tourism, Paris.

KLAUS WEIERMAIR

Tourism Development and Entrepreneurship

The entrepreneur and entrepreneurship must be considered the most critical resource for the creation, growth, decline and market exit of business firms. This is not different in tourism; if anything it is heightened by the fact that in most OECD jurisdictions over 70 % of all tourism enterprises constitute small sized owner managed firms where the entrepreneur is the most important and/or most critical resource. At the same time we can observe stylized patterns of life cycles in terms of birth, growth, decline and exit at all levels of aggregation from the life cycle of the individual entrepreneur, to the enterprise to the industry or branch of economic activity and finally to the product. While there has been a considerable amount of discussion regarding the life cycle of tourism destinations (Butler, 2006) relatively little has been written regarding the life cycle of the tourism industry or the life cycle of tourism enterprises and tourism entrepreneurs and their inter-relationship (Russel, 2006).

Before analyzing specific case studies of innovative entrepreneurs chosen among OECD jurisdictions it might be useful at the outset to describe typical patterns of inter-relationship between entrepreneur-, firm-, destination- and industry life cycles to be observed and/or expected in tourism.

The very first economic application of a life cycle is associated with the product life cycles pioneered by Vernon (1966) which illustrates the creation, growth, decline and economic death of a given and unchanged product as a demand phenomenon and under the rather restrictive assumption of unchanging product, production and- marketing conditions. Because, to remember, every effort by entrepreneurs or management to rejuvenate or reengineer products would constitute the establishment of an entirely new product life cycle.

Keeping this caveat in mind we now apply the life cycle concept to the tourist destination and the tourism industry and compare it with the entrepreneurial and enterprise life cycle in tourism (or generally speaking with entrepreneurship in tourism).

Depending on tourists' perceptions a destination can vary from a resort or village to regions, countries or even constitute a whole continent. Concentrating on the resort or village (city) as the typical tourist destination one captures not only the most dominant perception of a tourist' destination but also comes close to the notion of the existence of "a destination product" subject to the forementioned life cycle. If we use more aggregate destination entities such as regions or entire countries we involve an entire tourism industry of a country. The destination life cycle is said to involve 6 phases e.g. exploration, involvement, development, consolidation, stagnation and decline (or rejuvenation). Together they create a stylized S growth curve, as shown in figure 1 and where the exact position and shape of the PLC are determined by the size and strength of the driving forces behind each of the 6 life cycle phases.

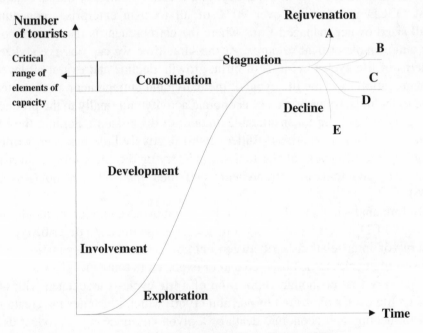

Figure 1: Destination Life Cycle (Butler, 1980)

In the aggregate of an entire country or the entire tourism industry a similar though drawn out life cycle (or growth curve) exists which consists of tourism product portfolios rather than individual tourism products and which displays somewhat similar features. The tourism industry cycle starts invariably with nature based and/or cultural heritage products produced and marketed at a small scale which subsequently become exploited and commercialized in the take up/growth phase and which became subject to both natural capacity utilization limits and economic predictions in the consolidation/stagnation phase. By then the industry requires newer, more innovative products and services frequently imported from other sectors of economic activity. Where the entire tourism industry in specific regions and jurisdictions is based on very few and standardized single and/or simple tourism products, the tourism product-, destination- and industry life cycle are very similar if not synonymous in both nature and (short) duration. Cases in point are water bound or sea side regions and/or islands offering simple beach vacation and or alpine summer resorts offering simple products such as hiking and nature at average market prices. On the other hand a much flatter drawn out and (long term) industry/destination life cycle is involved if the tourism industry (but also destinations encompassing a whole country) possess either very unique tourist attractions or a strongly diversified portfolio of different natural and man made tourist attractions which in some cases could even be altered on account of shifting tourism demand. Cases in point are health and educational tourism or city tourism. The relationship between the underlying tourism product life cycle and the associated destination and/or tourism industry life-cycle under these two regimes in stylized form looks as follows:

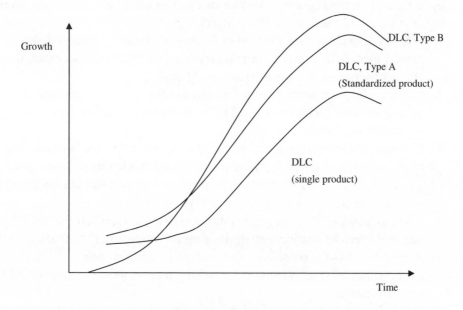

Figure 2: Different types of DLCs

The best way to understand innovative entrepreneurship in tourism is to view it in the context of the destination life cycle (Weiermair et al; Peters and Weiermair, 2001). Among the six destination cycle phases of discovery, introduction, take off, consolidation, maturity and stagnation there are three in which entrepreneurship plays a crucial role. In two of these phases e.g. discovery and maturity, innovative entrepreneurship creates the dynamic stimulus for the direction of further destination development while in the take off growth phase entrepreneurs are typically only concerned with the mechanic and rapid expansion of successful business concepts, thus laying the foundation for the coming destination turning points towards maturity and decline. Probably the most interesting phase for innovation and entrepreneurship occurs after potential resorts or destinations have been discovered, hence the demand side has signalled viability for tourism development and it now depends on the existence of local (or in some cases international) entrepreneurs to correctly interpret customers' (tourists') wants and/or preferences and to act upon it. True "Schumpeterian" entrepreneurship (Schumpeter, 1968) is required to visualize and develop tourism products/services or a "tourism experience" based on scanty and prelimary (evidence) from a few adventure travellers (De, 2005). In the case of most developed countries seaside and alpine vacation tourism was started in the primary sectors of agriculture and/or fishing. For nature based tourism and destinations to become developed through entrepreneurs a number of environmental conditions are likely to act as potential catalysts and/or barriers, e.g.:

1. Where only subsistence farming or fishing and petty entrepreneurship prevail there is little drive towards creating new types of businesses, including tourism (e.g. in many parts of Africa)
2. If successful local entrepreneurs are already present in the primary or other economic sectors there will be a greater likelihood of them entering the tourism industry.
3. The more diversified an economic region is with respect to its endowment of resources as required for the production and marketing of tourism services the easier it will be for entrepreneurs to set up business in new fields of economic activity such as e.g. tourism.
4. Local availability of entrepreneurship and risk capital determine the initial size and speed of tourism and destination development. If both are absent there still exists the possibility that foreign investment and – entrepreneurship can substitute for lacking local resources. (e.g. underdeveloped regions)
5. Generally ideal conditions for innovative entrepreneurship in the destination discovery and -take off phase are those which provide entry barriers which are neither too high nor too low e.g. creating the right level of risk and risk return, which mobilizes entrepreneurs (Walder, 2006).

6. Irrespective of local market conditions, there exists another possibility through the immigration of entrepreneurial talent, creating new tourism businesses (e.g. early alpine tourism in Canada, the U.S.A or Australia).

Entrepreneurship associated with the subsequent take off and growth phase of the destination life cycle (often also associated with the development of large scale or mass tourism) is usually much less innovation oriented and more concerned with the procurement of large scale financing required for growth. The preponderance of financial entrepreneurship when coupled with a neglect for the development of new business models and a strategic reorientation of existing products, services and markets often contributes to pushing tourism enterprises and destinations into the maturity and stagnation phase of the destination life cycle.

Once in the maturity or beginning stagnation phase of the life cycle most destinations in order to rejuvenate and/or reengineer themselves require again the rise of the innovative entrepreneur who can help reorient destinations out of old products and/or services into creating new tourism processes and services for existing or new markets (Cooper, 2005). Typically the environmental context for entrepreneurship in mature markets/destinations has again changed so that a number of propositions can be made with respect to the rise and fall of innovative entrepreneurship e.g.

- Tourism enterprises and tourism destinations which have in the past grown through continuously innovating new products, processes, organisations or markets will likely not easily reach maturity and stagnation and if for some reasons they do, they will very quickly reengineer themselves through "entrepreneurship" into new successful business ventures.
- At the other extreme conservative owner managed tourism enterprises which have never departed from their original business concept over the past 50 Years and who have served a loyal and equally conservative (today dying) customer segment are much less likely to initiate entrepreneurial activities aimed at "creative destruction of traditional business practices" (Schumpeter, 1968). Entrepreneurship and enterprises in such market conditions typically have a life cycle of their own which follow and indeed may even drive the market based product life cycle as shown below in figure 3.
- Where maturity is short lived and rather steep, and stagnation comes in the form of an economic crisis in tourism (or other key regional economic sector) there is a greater likelihood for destinations to rejuvenate through entrepreneurship (see e.g. the transformation of the two out-

23

dated or mature industrial ports, Bilbao and Glasgow,) into service and tourism centres.

- Finally there is, particularly in times of market saturation and high levels of competition with traditional tourism products/services the window of opportunity for market entry into tourism markets with novel tourism services/experiences by firms who can build new synergies between their core product/core competences (often stemming from an industrial base) and add soft and human ware components in order to create novel products which frequently also require novel or innovative production or marketing practices and techniques.

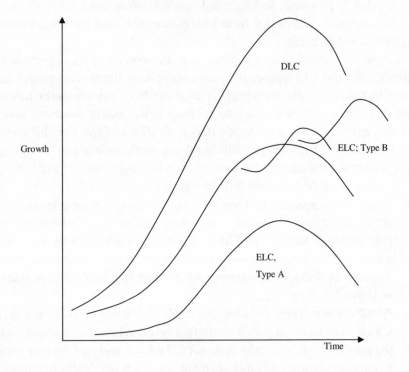

Figure 3: Pairs of type A and B of tourism destination and tourism enterprise life cycles

Having described theoretical/conceptual conditions &characteristics for innovative entrepreneurship the next section will provide actual cases of typical innovative entrepreneurship in tourism selected on the basis of identical criteria across nine countries with greatly varying market conditions.

References

Butler, R. (2006), The Origins of the Tourism Area Life Cycle, in: Butler, R. (Ed.) The Tourism Area Life Cycle Vol. 1, Channel View Publications, Clevedon, 13–26.

Cooper, C. (2005), Tourism – Principles and Practice, in: Harlow. Pearson Education.

De, D. (2005), Entrepreneurship – Gründung und Wachstum von kleinen und mittleren Unternehmen. München, Pearson Studium.

Russell, R(oslyn) (2006), The Contribution of Entrepreneurship Theory to the TALC Model, in: Butler, R (Ed.) The Tourism Area Life Cycle Vol. 2, Channel View Publications, Clevedon, 105–123.

Schumpeter, J. (1968), The Theory of Economic Development, Cambridge, Harvard Univ. Press.

Vernon, R. (1966), International Investment and international trade in the product life cycle, in: Quarterly Journal of Economics, 80, Issue 2, 190–207.

Walder, B. (2006), Sources and determinants of innovation – the role of market forces, in: Walder, B, et al (eds.) Innovation and Product Development in Tourism, ESV, Berlin, 7–24.

KLAUS WEIERMAIR AND CHRISTOPHER KRONENBERG

Moving from Traditional Tourist Products to Cultural Tourism Experience – The Case of Swarovski Crystal Worlds

1.   Introduction – Background Swarovski

Swarovski is the world's leading manufacturer of cut crystal. This Austrian family company which goes back more than 100 years is globally recognized for their products, especially for crystal products. Daniel Swarovski I, founder of the company was a man of ingenuity, imagination and uncompromising standards. He was born in Central Europe and into the golden era of stunning radical artistic movements of the Seccession and Wiener Werkstätte. He moved from Bohemia to Tyrol, Austria in 1895, bringing with him two things – his special invention for cutting crystal with previously unknown precision and a desire to "constantly improve on what was the going know how and quality of the time".

1892	29-year-old Daniel Swarovski invents an industrial device for cutting crystal jewellery stones with unsurpassed perfection and precision.
1895	Daniel Swarovski moves with his family from Georgenthal in Boehemia to Wattens in the Tyrol/Austrian, a center of jewellery stone production since the early 18th century.
1913	Together with his three sons, Wilhelm, Friedrich and Alfred, Daniel Swarovski establishes a crystal production plant in which he can produce his own purest quality raw material. To this day the company's success has been due to its uncompromising quality standards.
1919	Swarovski markets grinding wheels under the registered trade name of TYROLIT. TYROLIT is the leading supplier of grinding wheels today and one of the three largest suppliers in the world.
1937	Retroflection studs and pavement markers have been introduced into the market as a world novelty in road safety products.

1948	The Swarovski Optic factory is established. Under the registered trade name of HABICHT Swarovski's optical instruments, telescopes, sniper scopes and binoculars gain a leading position in world markets.
1960	Swarovski founds its first sales company in Germany. Today over 40 sales companies are responsible for the distribution of Swarovski products throughout the world.
1975	Swarovski's new "Hotfix"-technology makes it possible to iron crystal on to fabrics. Prefabricated designs, known as "Transfers", are launched soon thereafter.
1976	The success story of the world of the Swarovski brand begins with a tiny crystal mouse, which is soon followed by other lifelike animal figurines. Today the collection incorporates more than 120 gift items and collectibles. The brilliant cut crystal figurines depict themes from the world of fauna and flora, childhood memories and Christmas themes. They are available in over 160 company owned stores as well as in more than 9,000 retail outlets around the world.
1987	The Swarovski Collectors Society (SCS) is founded with the aim of offering crystal devotees special services and a communication platform. The members, who today number over 430,000, enjoy special privileges such as the opportunity to purchase annual limited editions of specially produced collectors' pieces, as well as the Swarovski magazine, which appears four times a year.
1995	As the culmination of its centenary year, in October Swarovski opens the Swarovski Crystal Worlds, created by the Austrian artist André Heller, in Wattens, Tyrol. In this architectonically unique construction shaped like a botanic giant, the magical world of crystal can be experienced in a space covering over 4000 square meters. Works of art and fantastic installations convey the diverse beauty of crystal.

Today – more than 100 years later and in the hands of the fourth and fifth family generation – the company still pursues its founder's philosophy and vision in its products and services.

2.   Swarovski Crystal Worlds

In 1995 Swarovski commissioned André Heller to create a permanent symbol of the magic of crystal and to facilitate a novel cultural/spiritual/aesthetic experience for Swarovski customers and non-customers. This permanent show was also established to celebrate the company's first century of achievement. The Crystal Worlds cover now an area of 4000 square meters near Swarovski's permanent headquarters. Swarovski Crystal Worlds presents crystals and works of art and installations. To date over 6 million visitors (tourists) have visited the Crystal Worlds in Tyrol.

3.   Product Development and Innovations

Swarovski has always embarked on a differentiation strategy. That means that Swarovski has always tried to create products which are unique or which create new services that are perceived as being unique. The company's strategy is also to focuses on market niches. These market segments could be a particular buyer group (e.g. the Swarovski Collectors Society), a special service (e.g. the Crystal Worlds as unique tourism attraction) or a unique product (e.g. crystal, TYROLIT). In general differentiation and focus strategies allow the firm to command a higher price because of the uniqueness of products and / or service on the market. Swarovski's key innovation forces were market as well as company internal driven. Daniel Swarovski, founder of the company, was led by his ideas to produce crystal jewellery stones with unsurpassed perfection and precision. For this goal he and his sons also developed special grinding wheels for in-house use. These grinding wheels, registered under the trade name TYROLIT which is today the leading supplier in Europe and one of the three largest suppliers in the world.

The Swarovski Crystal Worlds were created to celebrate the anniversary of the company but also to create a unique architectural construction to present the company's famous products. Today the magical world of crystal is also one of the most important tourism attractions in Tyrol.

4.   Entrepreneurial Vision

Impetus for the innovation was the collectors club which needed a new product or service ideas as well as the anniversary of Swarovski, and market pull forces in terms of the need for experience products. Swarovski was the first to realise the potential to add value to tourism products (crystal products) through the creation of a new product in the form of an experience allowing people to escape every day life and submerge into a fantasy / spiritual world of novel experiences which where themed along cultural and material (crystal) dimensions. This vision was based on an understanding of changing customer (tourist) motivation towards increased individualisation, experience orientation, spiritualism and recognition of a global market for these enhancing needs of tourists. What was essentially a product innovation also required an organisational innovation (Anthony et al., 2006) providing through Crystal

Worlds a new organisational platform across which a new corporate identity could be forged on all stakeholders in the company.

A further associated innovative change has been in the field of marketing. Swarovski was the first who moved from simple forms of sales promotion on to new forms of marketing through entrepreneurial networks, cooperative networks and co branding (Morrison et al, 2004). Challenge for the future is the location and market limitations which the firm is however overcoming through continuing provision of new products, services, shows and events with new artists and newly staged experiences. Expansions into new and globally co branded products and locations are planned. Today over 720.000 tourists visit the crystal worlds per year. In the future it is planned to work more closely with architects and artists. Similarly the firm is looking out for new partners for capitalizing on cultural change and / or new forms of experiential products and services (Pine, 1999).

References

Anthony, S., Eyring, M. and Gibson, L. (2006), Mapping Your Innovation Strategy, in: Harvard Business Review, Vol. 84, No. 5, pp. 104–113.

Morrison, A., Lynch, P., Johns, N. (2004), International Tourism Networks, in: International Journal of Contemporary Hospitality Management, Vol. 16, No. 3, pp. 198–204.

Pine, J., J. Gilmore (1999), The experience economy, Harvard Business School Press, Boston.

LUIZ GONZAGA GODOI TRIGO

Handling the Volatile Demand – The CVC Tour Operator Case in Brazil

The case illustrates as to how the volatility of the market (international and domestic) affected the tourism-related businesses in Brazil for the last two decades. A large number of Brazilian tour operators suffered due to an internal economic crisis, international economic situations and the terrorist attacks after September 11, 2001. Several companies went bankrupt and some managed to survive but one of them reached an absolute preponderance in the national market, becoming the biggest tour operator in Brazil and also one of the most influential tourism companies in the country: CVC. It was born as a small company that only operated with buses in 1972. Today it is a structure of 136 stores throughout the country, 800 employees and it served 1.1 million passengers between January and October of 2005. This text analyses its history, its business strategy that made its leadership possible in a very unstable country, and the tactics and current policies that will allow the maintenance or growth of its activities.

1   Introduction

According to official statistics and data from the tourism companies, tourism in Brazil has been growing considerably for the past fifteen years (www.turismo.gov.br). Both, the public and private sectors have invested in many areas such as: hospitality, transportation, food & beverage, entertainment and tourism operation (in general). As a developing country with a recent democratic regime (since 1985), Brazil deeply felt the economic and cultural changes (globally speaking) of the last 30 years. Many companies went bankrupt and others growth taking advantage of the euphoria/depression cycle that the Brazilian economy presented during this period. The volatility was considerable in the economy as much as in the tourism industry. Planners and managers took many decisions which in many cases were taken without a reliable information or social/political safety and, in the middle of periodic economic crises. In the middle of this political and economical chaos, a tour operator became absolutely preponderant in the business, dominating around 70 % of the domestic Brazilian market in 2005. In order to understand the reasons that led CVC to this indubitable success in the first decade of the 21st Century, it is necessary to understand the economic (recent) history of Brazil.

2   Adjusting the Accounts

For the first time in its history Brazil presents a positive Balance of Trades and it favorably affects the tourism industry. During the last years (2003/2004) the Brazilian Balance of Trade has been positive, as well as the account "International Trips". These results were partially enabled by a better exchange rate (Real in relation to the American Dollar and to the Euro).

Year	Exchange Rate BRL/USD Average (month)	Revenue/Expense USD millions USD millions		Balance USD millions
1995	0,92	971,6	3.391,3	-2.419,70
1996	1,00	839,8	4.438,3	-3.598,50
1997	1,08	1.060,0	5.445,8	-4.376,80
1998	1,16	1.585,7	5.731,7	-4.146,00
1999	1,82	1.628,2	3.085,3	-1.457,10
2000	1,83	1.809,9	3.894,1	-2.084,20
2001	2,35	1.730,6	3.198,6	-1.468,00
2002	2,92	1.998,0	2.395,8	- 397,80
2003	3,08	2.478,7	2.261,1	217,60
2004	3,03	3.222,1	2.871,3	350,80

Source: Brazilian Central Bank, IMF, Ipeadata

Table 1: Account "International Trips"

These data clearly show us that since the dollar crisis (1999), with the Brazilian currency *"real"* devaluing, there was a significant decrease in the number of international trips, that was a bit recovered in the middle of the year 2005 (data still not consolidated) with the Real currency getting stronger. The dollar stabilization (around BRL 2,50) in 2005 (and BRL 2,15 in the beginning of 2006) favored exports and influenced positively the Balance of Payments. It was in this scenario (so complex and conflicting) that **CVC Tour Operator** found itself in a favorable environment which made its development even more fortunate.

3   Brazilian Economic and Political Problems

Brazil has been through major changes since the 1980s. It is necessary to understand this context of economic, political and social evolution in order to be able to interpret changes in the specific field of tourism.

Brazil's political history covers: the colonial period (1500–1822) when the country was Portugal's colony; after the independence (September 07, 1822) there was a Brazilian Empire (1822–1889), the first Republic (1889–1930) and the "so called" *Getúlio Vargas* Era (1930–1945) – a strong populist civil dictatorship; the short democratic period between 1946 and 1964; the Military Dictatorship, from 1969 to 1985 and the recent Republic from 1985 on, with a regime of consolidated and stable democratic rights. The period that interests here is the last one. The period of redemocratization (since 1985) lead to:

- economic opening (international capital);
- social reliability in relation to the democratic stabilization;
- new laws and a new Constitution (1988);
- international investment, including the areas of entertainment, hotel management and food & beverage;
- strengthening of political bonds with South American countries;
- a beginning of relations with countries such as: India, China, Russia, Arabian Countries and Africa;
- a bigger transparency in some aspects like corruption and organized crimes (all of this, thanks to the media);
- an awareness of a need to deepen the tributary, legal and political reforms.

The recent economic history of Brazil has been extremely confusing. A cruel mark of this economic crisis, since 1960, was the inflation. The military regime left an accumulated inflation, between 1964 and 1985 of 977,251.9 %. In order to control this incredible cycle, 4 civil presidents (from the 1980s and 1990s) launched 5 economic plans.

Plan	President	Period
Plano Cruzado	José Sarney	February 1986
Pano Cruzado 2	José Sarney	November 1986
Plano Bresser	José Sarney	April 1987
Plano Collor	Fernando Collor	March 1990 to 1991
Plano Real	Itamar Franco	1993/1994

Obs. The "*Plano Real*" was idealized by Fernando Henrique Cardoso, Itamar Franco's head of the Treasure Department and after – Brazil's president from 1995 to 2002.

Table 2: Brazilian Economic Plans

This sequence of economic plans had as its main objective to control the inflation. The inflation control is something new in Brazil. More than a decade separates the military regime (appointed by uncertainty and a necessity of consecutive personal and institutional plans) from the economic stability era and the political legality. The success of the stability in the economic field was neither easy nor quick. In 1992, for example, only four countries in the world had an inflation of over 1,000 %: Russia, Ukraine, Zaire and Brazil. The first three had their economies compromised, taking into account that Russia and Ukraine were in a difficult process of transition from socialism to a market economy. The problem in Brazil was a huge state deficit, a culture of instability and a market of a financial vicious circle difficult to be banned. The economic scenario was so uncertain that the country had seven different currencies in a period of fifty years.

Despite the political and economic instability, throughout the 1990s several international political and financial crises came up. This situation of uncertainty since 1999 has been provoking a contradictory feeling in Brazil of fear and euphoria. The fears are because of the economic crisis trauma marked by the inflation and income concentration. There was a bad feeling towards the possibility of inflation returning and the impossibility of planning for a medium and long term basis. The feeling of euphoria was due to the situation of neutrality of the country in the international scenario and the fact that Brazil was free of terrorism (despite its misery, social injustice and urban violence in big cities). At the same time the country was facing the insertion into the international market (Ricupero, 2001) and the globalization effects (Soros, 2003; Stiglitz, 2002) and was also positioning itself as a very attrative destination to international tourists. The election of Luis Inácio Lula da Silva, in 2003, provoked a transitory instability, soon softened by the fact that the new president would keep orthodox economic politics.

The strong economic crisis in 2005, motivated by corruption accusations involving the executive and legislative powers, and an economy of high interest levels of the federal government left marks in the economy. The growth was not what it was expected at first (around 6 % a year), maybe it will be less than 3 %, a shy mark in relation to other developing countries. Despite all of this there were some social developments and the political stability remains.

These facts have caused many transformations in the tourism industries throughout the 1990s. The airline companies – Vasp and Transbrasil – went bankrupt after a long process that did not end in the juridical field only. Varig, a traditional Brazilian airline company is going through a crisis that has never been seen before and it did not go bankrupt because the Brazilian government indirectly helped the company. TAM airlines, created in 1975 and GOL, 2001, have become the biggest airline companies in the national market and Varig sustained its domination in the international market (Trigo, 2002).

The hotel industry has had a fantastic progress in the country. National and international chains (Accor, Atlantica, Blue Tree, Sol Meliá, Marriott, Pestana, Othon), have grown in the last decade at a 7 % annual rate. Nowadays cities like São Paulo, Curitiba, Brasília, and Belo Horizonte have a surplus of hotel rooms. They offer low room rates and the competition is almost destructive, due to a badly planned expansion and distribution in the units of the hotel and in other forms of accommodation – the flats – a typical Brazilian product. These questions are not going to be discussed since they are not the focus of this case.

4   The Tour Operator Segment in Brazil

The bibliography about tour operators in Brazil and travel agencies is almost nonexistent (Duarte, 1998; Gadzanis, 2002; Trigo, 2002; Tomelin, 2001 and 2005; Beni, 2003), and some of these texts are simply chronological descriptions (Trigo, 2002) or exclusive to the market (Beni, 2003).

Brazilian tour operators possess an association called *Associação Brasileira das Operadoras de Turismo (Braztoa* – Brazilian Association of Tour Operators) that was created in 1989 (www.braztoa.com.br). It assembles 61 operators: 53 in the state of São Paulo, 4 in Rio de Janeiro, 1 in Espírito Santo, 1 in Alagoas, 1 in Paraná and 1 in Bahia. The associated operators are responsible for more that 85 % of the businesses – national and international packages and also for the issuing of 12 % of the total of air tickets in Brazil (2005 data). This association does not have periodical or permanent publications. The Ministry for Tourism in Brazil presents some statistical analysis related to the field (www.turismo.gov.br).

As the bibliography is rare and the statistics are limited (about this subject), this work is based on primary sources from the internet, the press and interviews, specially with CVC leaders.

The market of tour operators in Brazil is dominated by Brazilian entrepeneurs. In the 1970s and 1980s European Operators such as Abreutur (Portugal), Meliá (Spain), Paneuropa (Portugal) and Polvani (Italy) owned important segments in the national market and survived the economic instability thanks to their income in American dollars. Throughout the economic plans, currency changes and arbitrary measures from the military regime in relation to the tourism industry, these operators headquartered in Europe, had the dollar as a solid reference to their businesses in Brazil. Due to legal circumstances *(Gecam notice* 313 from June 10, 1976 from Brazil Central Bank, for example), travel agencies and tour operators had to work in an "illegal system" sending large quantities of dollars abroad. Brazil was a "closed" country, Brazilians did not have international credit cards and this *Gecam notice* 313 also did not allow the remitting of foreign currency to other countries. Hence, there was a network of agencies that operated in the black market which had support through the corruption that was almost completely institutionalized. In this absolutely unusual and absurd situation international operators managed to survive, despite the low number of people who traveled abroad. Some Brazilian operators specialized in national packages and risked on their own selling some trips to foreign countries, basically to the USA and Europe.

Since the 1990s foreign operators have noticed that such an unstable market (which was influenced by not always transparent issues) was no longer attractive: their activities were reduced and they became irrelevant in the wide, prosperous post 1995 market. Some national operators, which progressed even more thanks to international trips, overcame the tough uncontrolled inflation years in Brazil but dissapeared due to the 1999 financial crisis and 9/11.

One of the first Brazilian tour operators in Brazil to start its businesses in foreign countries was *Stella Barros Turismo*. Founded in 1965, it was specialized in flying tourists to Florida, soon after Walt Disney World's opening in 1971. The company developed and was sold to Citibank at the end of the 1980s. Its problems started in 1998 with the World Cup (soccer) in Paris. Due to management problems (never explained to the public) the company only sold 2,750 tickets from the 3,600 tickets paid to the public. A fact that caused indignation with Brazilian people, who came to Paris to watch the final game of the World Cup (won by France). The *Real* currency devaluation, in 1999 and 9/11 only worsen the problems for the company as Brazilians started to travel even less abroad. Stella Barros Turismo went bankrupt (asked for it) on December 13, 2003, through its controller in the USA, *Travel Ya* (connected to the Citibank). Centered in the external market, the operator could not resist the change of the century (*Isto É Dinheiro Magazine*, February 19, 2003). Its 23 franchise stores were suddenly alone and unarticulated. Only a few survived.

Something similar happened to *Soletur* (a Brazilian tour operator as well). On October 24, 2001 the company (that was 38 years old) with 450 employees, went bankrupt and closed its doors leaving the market completely startled. Soletur has started its activities as a very successful land (bus) operator. Little by little it expanded its business to Paraguay, Uruguay, Argentina and Chile and further on to North America, Europe, South Africa and Asia/Oceania. At the beginning of the 21st Century around 70 % of its revenue depended upon the sales of international trips, a contrary position in relation to its origins and also to CVC's origins that favored domestic trips. Some reasons for its bankruptcy are clear and similar to the Stella Barros's ones: Real's devaluation in 1999, international terrorism in 2001 and the decline of international trips. Other reasons were not clearly explained. There were some rumors on the internet about a letter from Soletur's managers' blaming VARIG. According to this rumor it was a deceitful action by Varig to rush the process of Soletur's bankruptcy. The truth is that in 2000 and 2001, Soletur was making bets on the American winter in order to sell packages at very reasonable prices, especially to New York and Miami. Then, 9/11 happened and its main sale strategy was compromised. Soletur and Stella Barros were 2 of the most known and important operators in Brazil.

One of the most "frightening" cases in the Brazilian tour operators market was Varig Travel, connected to Varig Airlines. Created in 2001, its dissolution was approved by an exceptional general assembly on October 31, 2003 by 92 % of its stockholders. Only a few articles about the subject were published by the Brazilian press (for example – Veja Magazine: February 11, 2005 issue number 1904, by Chrystiane Silva). This article reveals an estimated debt of around USD 18 million. Varig's history has many obscure details. It may have been protected by the military dictatorship in 1965 at the occasion of the *Pain Air do Brasil* bankruptcy. This case has never been explained, neither by the military government, nor by the civil government. A book was published 40 years later – *Pouso Forçado* ("Forced Landing") –

telling the story of Varig's interests on Pan Air's bankruptcy provoked by the military (Sasaki, 2005). It is one of the few documents telling this uncertain episode in the history of Brazilian aviation. In the context of Brazilian corporative mysteries involved with governmental bodies, the Varig Travel case was simply forgotten.

5   The CVC Case

CVC emerges as the leading tour operator in 2002 in the process of a constant and careful development. Its success is so new that there are almost no articles about the subject. This study has ultimate assistance by Virgílio Nélson da Silva Carvalho, advisor of CVC's president Guilherme Paulus. The archives of the companies were conceded to me and Virgílio Carvalho was the president's spokesperson in reference to the strategy and the tactics of the company in the Brazilian market.

Founded in 1972, in Santo André (a region of São Paulo state, close to São Paulo, known as "great São Paulo"), CVC possesses (2005) around 800 direct employees and 1600 indirect ones and 137 outlets in Brazil. A very different technique that the company used during its first years (1978) was the organization of traveler groups or bus trips. Those trips were mainly composed of groups of workers from the industrial regions of the state of São Paulo, thus they simply "started" the idea of organized mass tourism in the country. Throughout the 1980s the company began to operate with air packages. In 1989 CVC bought 100 thousand air tickets from VASP in order to resell them. This number represented 50 % of all monthly sales of the airline. The sales were very successful and the operation became known as a marketing case of Brazilian tourism. In October 1992 CVC chartered, for the first time, planes for the private use of its passengers. The first destinations were Maceió, Natal, Porto Seguro, Serra Gaúcha e Pousada do Rio Quente. In 1993 the packages to Aruba and Cancun were negotiated with extensive advertisement. Its sales and operational program called "Systur" was already connecting 670 terminals (travel agents) in the year 2000. Its detailed history is on the company website – www.cvc.com.br – including all the awards and honors.

CVC's mission is: *"Creating conditions of approaching the world of tourism to all levels of the Brazilian society with compatible quality and prices, maintaining the leadership and recognition of the market, generating employment and revenue, keeping, achieving and enchanting clients and suppliers".*

The company has recently acquired hotels in Brazil. Only a few units have been bought but there is a development perspective. There also exists an alliance with *"Pullman Tur"*, owner of the ship *"Blue Dream"* chartered by CVC, a fact that really makes the tourism industry (from Brazil, Uruguay and Argentina) more diversified.

CVC has already transported around 7.5 million passengers and its distribution network reaches seven thousand travel agents in 23 of the 26 Brazilian states. Its growth, in 2004, was of 38 % over 2003 and it was kept in 2005: exceptional numbers in any world-wide market (Case Studies, May/June 2005). CVC is still smaller than TUI, for example, which has a movement of around 8 million passengers/year but Germany is one of the countries that sends more tourists abroad and with a population of high income. In relation to the Brazilian market CVC numbers are excellent ones:

YEAR	Transported Passengers by CVC (National and International)
2002	572,910
2003	696,548
2004	1,040,000
2005	1,472,000
2006	1,800,000 (estimated)
Source - (CVC – São Paulo)	

Table 3: Transported Passengers

Interviews, political analysis and the company's projection were abridged in 12 topics that allow the reader to understand the reason(s) why CVC has become the leader in such an extreme, volatile market. This is a market where foreign companies were taken away and powerful national operators went bankrupt at the turn of the century, without having conditions to face the systematic currency exchange rates and the new international scenario.

1. CVC does not sell more than 20 % to the international market, so it will not make debts in dollar in the case of a currency exchange instability or international speculative attacks. When CVC started to make some progress, the international market was dominated by other operators and the company (pragmatically) invested in Brazilian tourism operating through land (bus). In the 1980s CVC started to operate with flights and it is today the leader in the prosperous segment of cruises, with 3 chartered ships employed during the Brazilian summer.

2. CVC adapted the consumer's dreams according to their reality trough 3 characteristics: fair prices, thanks to transactions with suppliers (large scale); long-term financing (10 months) without interest, something very attrative in a country marked by an old trauma of inflation; using the economic stability from the last years as an incentive, so that people can buy packages without worrying about unexpected economic problems.

3. Tourism preferences anticipated for the next season through computer based research. The company's database has 8 million clients. Through market segmentation it can prevent itself from occasional declines and increases on its destinations and make reservations for new charters. Some cities in the northeast of Brazil had a significant growth of visitors due to CVC's new packages.

4. The chartered flights created accessibility for a great number of clients that did not use planes. In Brazil air tickets are still expensive and this kind of transportation is seen reserved to the "leading circles of the society", thus unattainable to the "masses". Between December 2005 and February 2006 the company chartered 20 flights, on a weekly basis and hopes to achieve 50 thousand clients on its 3 ships that will be on the Brazilian coast for periods after the high season (summer). Its reservations are guaranteed by payments and contracts that are very well settled with airline companies. In 2004, 5,200 buses were chartered and 207,949 passengers transported (land). Around 6 % of TAM (Airline company) revenue comes from CVC's charters: a remarkable percentage that reinforces a partnership that is growing stronger and stronger.

5. It is a company that makes decisions quickly. Guilherme Paulus, his wife Luiza Paulus and Valter Patriani decide the long and short term measures, this fact avoids long delays that, in countries like Brazil, can be fatal due to the dynamics and instability that may occur because of the political or economical crisis, specially the ones generated in other countries.

6. CVC helped to break the pattern that tourism is something expensive and luxury. The company creates awareness; especially for people with low income that trips are good reasons for people to restore their physical capacity. To the society, CVC conveys the message that tourism can be a good option for generating income and employment. In a country where areas such as tourism, hotel management, gastronomy and entertainment are still seen with a certain kind of prejudice or are simply ignored, this massage may bring benefits, in the sense of creating new clients and making the old ones loyal.

7. Extremely advanced technology in all its operations. CVC uses Linux system, has a portal for its suppliers and one for its travel agents, as well as an online agency for its direct clients (www.cvc.com.br).

8. The company does not deal with businesses if there is a risk of not delivering the product (World Cup, Olympic Games, some shows, etc...). If there is not the possibility of total operational control, with absolute guarantee that the product will be delivered to the client, CVC does not close the deal (package or individual trip). In October, 2005, due to the hurricane that devastated Cancun, the company chartered a plane to get 110 Brazilian passengers who were still in Mexico and provided return transportation. This measure was done to insure a state of trustworthiness and safety to their clients.

9. There is strategic planning, structured in monthly meetings by the managers in order to plan and control its targets and discuses, occasional problems and opportunities. In an urgent case there are measures that come into action (decribed on item 5) where a small group of people promptly decides what should be done.

10. On a long term basis, CVC wants to become a retail company. It wants to be like a Wal Mart store for tourism. Nowadays some C&A stores and *Casas Bahia* (an enormous Brazilian chain of household appliances) already have sales of tourism-related products. Its economic packages are commercialized on TV and there are plans to reach C, D and E+ classes, the ones with an available income for leisure of around USD 30 a month. One of their inovative ideas was to open some stores inside Brazilian shopping malls. Brazilian middle classes often go to malls – shopping and to have all kinds of leisure. So it proofed a very successful idea for tourism market.

11. Focus on clients. The companies tend to know what the costumer wants and, most importantly, what he/she does not want or bothers them, their fears, biases and insecurities are researched and an afford is made to diminish all which prevent people from traveling whatever reason that may be (real or imaginary). This means that CVC organizes events to travel agents, such as seminars and workshops, in order to provide them with technical information and the company's philosophy.

12. They employ capable and engaged staff (in relation to the mentality of the company and its corporative values). A human resources policy is carried out to maintain the level of commitment. Annually, the company organizes a workshop (for thousands of travel agents) in order to make them aware of their products and marketing ideas.

6 Conclusions

This very expansive development raises questions regarding investment plan to their own airline, ships, hotels and restaurants. According to CVC's directors the company does not intend to cluster in the same pattern of "holding" like other companies causing a kind of "gigantism" that may be dangerous for their core business. Pan Am, Air France, Varig and American Airlines invested in hotel chains in the past with negative results, so an operator needs to know where to grow and to differ in order to avoid mistakes caused by the so-called "gigantism". Knowing that the German TUI and some Japanese operators have strong, consolidated policies in the market, CVC intends to keep in Brazil a sustainable development and avoid misfortunes caused by success. The positive side is that the company was ready to develop and make good use of the changing national and international environment. It is a conservative company whose power is concentrated in Guilherme Paulus, its main director.

Reaching more than half of the Brazilian market, the company became a case to be studied, especially because it was an important survival in a disastrous environment which crashed the finances of big Brazilian operators in a short 2-year period (between 2001 and 2003). Today some academic research (master degree's dissertations and MBA's case studies) are becoming preoccupied with the analysis of how this organizational development was so powerful and successful. It was probably a mixture of planning, development management, capacity, luck and quickness on making the best use of the opportunities that came along and which led these companies into the supremacy after 2001. Certainly CVC's past cannot be forgotten because these concepts and management qualities allowed a steady development (far from risks). The question remains as to whether its consumer will remain loyal. Several companies reached the top (Gross, 1997) and many, like Walt Disney World, a model of entertainment and tourism have been through major turbulences (Grover, 1992; Eisner, 1998; Thomas, 1998; Stewart, 2006). Other companies vanished throughout history and will not be remembered by future generations. The next years will be crucial to CVC. In a certain way, it needs to increase its international influence, for foreign tourists who visit Brazil or the ones that go to other countries. Because of that the branch in Argentina will be important, not only to arrange the arrival of Brazilians (who love going to Buenos Aires and Bariloche), but also to organize trips to the Argentineans (to Brazil) who love Brazilian beaches and cities. Of course it is not possible to guarantee that international operators (the larger ones) will not have an interest (in the medium or long term) for Brazil. Some airline companies, like TAM have their own operators and PNX Travel (another operator) is also developing and contesting the market. Competition is not what is lacking. On the other hand, it is hoped that Brazilian cyclical economic crises has already and definitively been left behind and today's stability may remain for a long time.

With an incitement for the global competition and the invigoration of the Brazilian tourism market, remaining on the top is becoming harder and harder. At the present time, judging by the numbers, the development presented and by the sincerity that the CVC directors present themselves to academic researchers and the press, the future scenario looks very promising. The next years will show us how correct the company and its position in the globalized world will be and whether the company can continue to remain innovative.

References

Beni, Mário. Globalização do turismo. São Paulo: Aleph, 2003.

Case Studies. Revista brasileira de Management. Rio de Janeiro: Maio/junho 2005.

Eisner, Michael. Work in progress. New York: Random House, 1998.

Gadzanis, T. Regulamentação da atividade. Anais do Congresso da ABAV. Recife, 2002.

Gross, Daniel. Forbes – Greatest Business Stories of all time. New York: John Wiley, 1996.

Grover, Ron. El toque mágico de Disney. México: McGraw-Hill, 1992.

Ricupero, Rubens. O Brasil e o dilema da globalização. São Paulo: Senac, 2001.

Sasaki, Daniel Leb. Pouso forçado. Rio de Janeiro: Record, 2005.

Schiffman, Leon G. e KANUK, Leslie L. Consumer behavior. New Jersey: Prentice Hall, 1994.

Ssoros, George. Globalização. Rio de Janeiro: Campus, 2003.

Stewart, James B. Disney War. Rio de Janeiro: Ediouro, 2006.

Stiglitz, Joseph. A globalização e seus malefícios. São Paulo: Futura, 2002.

Thomas, Bob. Building a company. New York: Hyperion,1998.

Tomelin, Carlos e Teixeira, Athos. Gerenciamento da cadeia de suprimentos e do marketing de relacionamento nas agências de viagens. In Trigo, Luiz G. G. "Análises regionais e globais do turismo brasileiro. São Paulo: Roca, 2005. pág. 685–709.

Tomelin, Carlos. Mercado de agencias de viagens e turismo. São Paulo: Aleph, 2001.

Trigo, Luiz G. G. Viagem na memória. São Paulo: Senac, 2002.

Veja (magazine). De 11/05/2002. São Paulo: Abril.

EILEEN FISCHER AND SAMIR MARKAREM

G.A.P Adventures[1] – A Successful Canadian Tourism Venture

G.A.P Adventures is a Canadian success story in the tourism sector. Founded nearly 15 years ago, this company has experienced success by focusing on an expanding niche, the adventure eco-tour market. In contrast with peer organizations, it has taken advantage of the Canadian image as a destination that offers unspoiled wilderness experiences without ever being dependent on it: despite its Canadian base, both the company's offerings and its clientele are broadly geographically based. This export orientation, combined with a steady innovation in terms of offerings, has led to strong and steady growth for G.A.P. Adventures.

1   Introduction

Tourism is currently one of the fastest growing industries in Canada, accounting for nearly two percent of the country's gross domestic product. Tourism supports close to 160,000 businesses in the country and employs more than half a million Canadians. In 2005 tourism in Canada generated over CAD 56 billion in economic activity (www.canadiantourism.com). Behind these statistics lie sweeping changes in the sector. In Canada as elsewhere, the globalization of trade has brought about competitive transformation across nearly every industry, and tourism has been no exception. As a result, the competition for tourist dollars is far from being local or domestic: travellers may compare and contrast tourism experiences on completely different continents when choosing their destination.

---

[1]   G.A.P stands for 'Great Adventure People. The company does not put a period after the "P"

Another significant change is the nature of the experience that tourists seek. The focus of the tourism industry and tour operators has shifted from the meeting needs for transportation, accommodation and food to providing total experiences or fantasy worlds associated with specific destinations (Koch, 1996). The paradigm of mass tourism, which was the norm for many decades, no longer suffices to achieve growth and competitiveness in the industry (Saayman, 1999).

In the face of changes both in terms of the explosion of competition and the evolution of tourists' tastes and preferences, how can entrepreneurs in the tourism industry compete? In particular, how can a Canadian based company find success given the many factors that make competing in Canada difficult? Canada's domestic population is a merger 32 million; many travellers from our largest trading partner and closest neighbour, the United States, have restricted their visits to foreign destinations since the events of 9/11/2001; Canada's image to foreign travellers is pleasant but extremely bland according to research on nations as brands (www.nationbrandindex.com); and the SARS crisis continues to lead many outside Canada to fear that there are previously unsuspected perils associated with travel to Canada.

The solution devised by entrepreneur Bruce Poon Tip, who founded and continues to manage G.A.P Adventures, appears to rest on three insights. First, pick a niche that is attractive to an emerging trans-national segment of travellers: small-group, adventure-based, eco- and culture-friendly, tourism. Second, develop a line of offerings that takes advantage of Canada's image but that is not confined to Canadian territory: adventure eco-tours in remote, naturally beautiful Canadian and non-Canadian locations. Third, keep finding or developing new offerings that take advantage of the company's image and expertise, but that allow for steady stream of new travel options for prior and new clients. Since being founded in 1991, G.A.P has been able to create a rewarding and lucrative tourism experience by maintaining its focus on these insights.

2 The Entrepreneur and His Vision

G.A.P's founder and CEO, Bruce Poon Tip, started out as a Calgary-born kid dreaming of an entrepreneurial future. While in high-school, he had experimented with money-making ventures outside the tourism sector. After high-school, Tip studied travel and tourism, and took a few business courses as well. However, Tip credits his first trip to Thailand in 1990, on a CAD 20 budget, as giving him the inspiration to pursue his vision of offering tours modelled on the his own experiences there.

The essence of the experience that Tip attempted to capture can be distilled into several elements. The first is an encounter with another setting or culture that is as authentic as is possible: it embraces and insists on exposure to the local people and their way of life, rather than offering insulation from it. The second is that it entails some element of out-door adventure, though not necessarily of a physically challenging kind: rather, it attempts to gain access to a setting that is off the beaten track and that possesses an unspoiled natural beauty compared with most conventional urban tour destinations. The third is that the experience is very social. Rather than an individual travelling alone or with a single other person, the experience Tip wanted to capture involves developing a sense of intimacy with like-minded others. Finally, it is consistent with an ethos of ecological sensitivity: rather than pampering and luxury, this experience emphasizes travel that does no harm to the planet and that may benefit the local hosts.

Although Tip's vision was clear, his timing had certain limitations. In 1991, the Canadian economy was in a significant slump, and Canadians were disinclined to devote significant resources to travel. These founding conditions may have proven to be a boon to the fledging company, however, as even from the start it did not look locally for either clients or destinations.

Equally fortunately, the Tip's vision can well be regarded, in retrospect, as a having been an act of insightful opportunity recognition. That is, the kind of tourism that Tip regarded as attractive and desirable corresponded to a demand that was yet to have become fully recognized or met in 1991. While tourism focusing on physical adventure and challenges had been provided for some years prior to 1991, particularly by British tour operators, the eco-adventure tour, with its emphasis on remote environments possessing natural beauty and rich cultural traditions represented an under-served market at this time (Walle 1997, Weber 2001).

G.A.P was also the insightful in tapping into a growing trend toward environmental and cultural sensitivity. Its emphasis on low impact tourism coupled with its philosophy of building relationships that support and benefit local hosts was timely given the growing interest, particularly among younger travellers, in sustainability and corporate social responsibility.

3   G.A.P Adventures Today

G.A.P Adventures is currently Canada's largest adventure travel company and a world leader in the adventure industry. It continues to offer unique small group adventures, with a focus on culture, nature and active travel. G.A.P differentiates itself from other tour operators by offering a varied 1000 adventure tours to over 100 countries on all 7 continents. Almost 40,000 passengers a year travel on small group adventures with G.A.P.

Building on its successes to date, the company is constantly seeking and exploring new destinations to bring new adventures to their customers. Unlike most tour operators, G.A.P creates its own training programs for local guides, porters and cooks who service the travel groups. G.A.P develops local experts rather than hiring local ground operators who often pay and treat their local employees poorly. This practice of developing local expertise is consistent with the company's developmental philosophy, and also helps it to maintain consistency in and some control over its service and travel experience.

G.A.P is also experimenting with new means of providing the kinds of experiences its clients seek. Earlier this decade, G.A.P decided to invest in operating assets and purchased the "Explorer", the world's first purpose-built expedition cruise ship. Today the Explorer covers routes in the Antarctic, the Amazon, and Greenland and has become a major success for the company. Indeed, this venture has been so successful for the company that in March of 2006, G.A.P. announced the acquisition of a second expedition ship, the M/S Andrea to allow it to meet the excess demand for trips to Antarctica program. "Acquiring M/S Andrea means G.A.P Adventures can now offer even more availability to meet the overwhelming demand for our Antarctic expeditions while continuing to offer the best prices in the market," said CEO Bruce Poon Tip.

G.A.P. has also engaged in some vertical integration, believing that this strategy is necessary in order to fuel rapid growth. In 2002, G.A.P doubled in size by making its first acquisition of Canada's largest flight consolidator to Latin America, Global Connections. Today G.A.P is able to offer highly competitive air travel in addition to its adventure tours.

G.A.P. is also experimenting with novel channels for reaching its clients and meeting their search needs effectively. While the company has a large interactive web site and call centre that serves clients, it is experimenting with store-fronts for travellers who seek to experience their potential choices and destinations in a more multi-sensory manner. In 2005, G.A.P opened two "Concept Stores" in high traffic areas in Toronto and Vancouver. Several more concept stores are in the works. These stores allow would-be travellers to research their own personal adventure trip and their favourite travel destinations without sales pressure. The stores have also become venues for music performances, multi-media travel presentations and lectures on travel-related topics.

G.A.P Adventures is also deeply engaged in a variety of non-profit organizations and community projects throughout the world, tangible evidence of its commitment to sustainability and corporate social responsibility. Most visibly, G.A.P established its own non-profit, the Planeterra Foundation. G.A.P Adventures pays all administration costs of the foundation and matches each donation dollar-for-dollar so that 100 % of each donation goes to support Planeterra projects. By identifying projects and organizations that specialize in different areas, donors to Planeterra are provided with a variety of worthwhile projects to choose from and support. This initiative reinforces it's positioning with its current and prospective clientele.

A measure of the success of G.A.P's strategies to date can be discerned from the list of awards and recognitions that the company, it products and its founder have garnered in recent years. In 2006, G.A.P. was selected from around thousands of applicants as one of Canada's 50 Best Managed Companies in a competition co-sponsored by a leading bank, newspaper and accounting firm in Canada. In this same year, it was ranked as one of Canada's Ten Best Employers for Young People. And Profit Magazine featured G.A.P Adventures in their annual ranking of the 50 fastest growing companies in Canada for five consecutive years. G.A.P Adventures was awarded the Premium Growth Award for appearing on the list for five straight years, the longest of any company.

On the product level, Outpost Magazine's annual Global Travel Guide ranked four of G.A.P's adventures in its 75 Great Adventures Guide for 2006. The following G.A.P Adventures trips were recognized: Ethiopia Simien Mountains, Brazil Tall Ship Adventure, Project Guatemala and Madagascar Adventure. And for three consecutive years starting in 2003, National Geographic Adventure Magazine has selected a G.A.P Adventures tour as one of the 25 Adventures of the Year.

The founder of G.A.P has also been recognized. For example, In 2002, Bruce Poon Tip was named the Canadian Entrepreneur of the Year by the National Post, Global Television and NASDAQ Exchange.

Perhaps most interesting given that G.A.P operates in the tourism sector is the exporting award that the company has obtained. In 2006, G.A.P was awarded the Ontario Government's Global Traders Market Expansion Award for growing its business through exporting. G.A.P Adventures was honoured with the gold level for this award which recognizes the most innovative and successful small and medium-sized exporters and business leaders throughout Ontario.

As this selection of awards suggests, there can be little doubt that the success of this venture stems from multiple factors. The core offering of the company meets well the needs of a sizable target market, and the company is committed to innovation in the services it provides and the ways that it provides them. Moreover, as with virtually all successful Canadian companies, there is no tendency to rely on local markets for growth.

References

Morrison, Alison, (2005), Entrepreneurship in tourism: moving from the generic to the particular, The Scottish Hotel School, University of Strathclyde.

Saayman, Melville (1999), Tourism Entrepreneurs: Opportunities And Threats. A South African Perspective, Institute for Tourism and Leisure Studies, Potchefstroom, South Africa.

Walle, A. H. (1997), Pursuing Risk or Insight: Marketing Adventures, in: Annals of Tourism Research 24:265–282.

Weber, Karin (2001), Outdoor Adventure Tourism: A Review of Research Approaches, in: Annals of Tourism Research, 28 (2), pp. 360–377.

Word Tourism Organization, WTO, (2005), Facts & Figures section at www.world-tourism.org.

www.canadatourism.com, May 2006.

http://www.deloitte.com/dtt/article/0,1002,sid %253D9078 %2526cid %253D106593,00.html, January 2006.

www.gapadventures.com, May 2006.

www.lesexplorers.com/50226711/gap_adventures_le_tour_operator_ecovoyages_et_aventures.php: Les Explorers: G.A.P Adventures : le Tour Operator eco-voyages et aventure, February 2006

http://www.travelandtransitions.com/interviews/bruce_poon_tip.htm

A Conversation with Bruce Poon Tip: Global Travel Entrepreneur with a Conscience, October 2005.

www.nationbrandindex.com/docs/GM_42606.pdf.

Raija Komppula

Touring Cars Finland LTD

1   The Business Idea

Touring Cars Finland (TCF) Ltd has been an innovator in camper rental operations in Northern Europe. The core idea of TCF is to rent a camper, based on a so called "Re-investment program". Through this program, an individual or a company can re-rent its camper to Touring Cars clients. The program gives multiple benefits to its members. Firstly, a monthly payment from TCF is paid regardless whether the company is able to rent a vehicle or not. Secondly, corporate clients can get VAT deduction and amortization benefits through the program. Thirdly, the program offers individuals an opportunity to rent out a camper without paying taxes on renting income. Fourthly, TCF maintains, cleans, checks-up each vehicle after every rental. Mandatory maintenances are performed, when necessary, during the rental season.

Today, the company has cooperative agreements with two mobile home manufacturers. They provide TCF with campers, which will be sold to private owners, and to be hired back to rental operation. The company mission is to offer unique travel experiences, to guarantee high service standards and customer satisfaction. Their corporate values are: trust, quality, customer satisfaction and experiences. According to their marketing message, when renting a camper, the customer gets a freedom to find the silence of the nature. It is not just renting a vehicle, but a high standard hotel room on wheels. They assist people from over 30 countries from four continents, with their goal of discovering Nordic and Baltic ways of living. (www.touringcars.fi)

Touring cars claim to be in business to sell emotions, experiences and life styles. Their promise is GOOD FEELINGS® to all of their customers, employees, and partners. The main travel product is a camper, which provides a KEY TO FREEDOM® for their clients. They emphasize needs of their clients but not their products. Their goal is to become a top five camper rental-company in the world. They also claim to be committed to environmental protection and ethical business processes. All this can be accomplished through collaboration among all stakeholders (www.touringcars.fi).

2   Touring Cars Finland Ltd, The History

Originally the company Touring Cars was founded in 1982 in Eastern Finland by an entrepreneur whose business was car sales and import. Current owner of the company, Ms Tanja Saarnio, started her job with the firm in 1989, when she was 23 years old and still studying at the university. Her mother used to work within the marketing department of a famous Finnish retailing chain and her father is an electrician. Brother of Tanja's grandfather was an entrepreneur and a supporter of a Russian school in Helsinki, which was the reason why Tanja attended to that school. There she learned the Russian language, which she later started to study as her major at the university. Tanja describes herself to have been a "creative but lazy school girl, who was interested in everything, not very diligent in her studies, but always found the school to be an easy job". She was active in sports, and participated in all the possible free time activities at the university.

During her studies she was invited by TC to help them in starting businesses in the Soviet Union. In the beginning she worked as interpreter and secretary. The aim of the Russian businesses was first to search for opportunities to manufacture motorhomes in Russia, but quickly it appeared not to be possible. Instead, because of Tanja's creativity and good knowledge of the Russian market and customer behaviour, combined with the entrepreneur's excellent skills in purchasing activities, the company found several kinds of new businesses in Russia, especially in retailing. In 1991 Tanja was designated as the managing director of the company.

During those years the company was concentrated in other fields of businesses in Russia, and the motorhome rental played a minor role. The company faced severe problems in the domestic market, and went bankrupt in 1993. Nevertheless, they had advertised their camper rental services and packaged tours, and had agreements with about 10 foreign tour-operators for the next season, but had no campers after the bankruptcy! Tanja managed to induce a former employee Jan to come back to the company, and after very complicated but innovative transactions they managed to hire used mobile homes from retailers, rent them out, and meet their commitments with the clientele.

1995 the original Touring Cars entrepreneur sold the motorhome business to Tanja, who decided not to continue any operations in Russia but to start a new page in the Touring Cars history. First of all she changed the name of the company to be Touring Cars Finland Ltd (TCF). In the beginning Tanja did not have any camper import or ownership of the motorhomes. During the first years she had 20–30 motorhomes for hire.

1996 Touring Cars Motorhome Ltd was established (TCM) to import Viva campers. 1998 they started to import Frankia motorhomes. Tanja's fundamental innovation was not to own the motorhomes but to hire them from private people or companies and then re-hire them out. Those days Tanja had a partner in TCM, and he was the one who invented the name for the system, "Re-Investment-program". He had visited a fair in Canada, from where he brought a picture of a motorhome and an example calculation. Actually, Tanja never got to know anything else but that name of this Canadian system, but these words gave her the fundamental idea of her own rental system. In Scandinavia this was a totally new business concept those days, and Tanja managed to develop her system without competition. Business was good: they imported motorhomes, sold them to private people, who hired them back to be hired out. The point was that their product was from the very beginning not only a "Rent a motorhome" but a "Key to Freedom": already in 1995 the first Key to Freedom booklet was published to serve clients to plan their trip.

In 1999, Tanja's mother started as marketing manager. In 2000 corporate sales increased 51 %, which was a substantial increase in general interest towards camping holidays. TCF started a reinvestment program with Solifer dealers and finished importing motorhomes. At the same time, Tanja bought her partner out and became a sole owner of the company. 2001 TCF opened its Oslo office after many requests from clients. The company also opened an office in Lakselv, which is the official airport location for North Cape, the northernmost point of continental Europe. Corporate sales increased by 9 %.

In 2002, despite the general down turn in the tourism industry due to 09/11, corporate sales increased by 25 %. TCF established its network wide training program, which included training manuals and training sessions for the camper owners and rental station stakeholders. The company became a member of national 1Q00 tourism enterprise quality program. In 2003 TCF bought out its franchisee in Stockholm, and started to manage the operations in Sweden. As a result, corporate sales grew substantially, total growth being 43 %. In the year of 2003, it was realised that the amount of online inquiries had been increasing steadily,so, a new web-site was opened to serve clients, who wanted to book directly online. The key to Freedom booklet was re-designed and distributed to more than 15 countries. TCF applied and received a Package Tour Operator license from The Finnish Consumer Agency. Once the application was approved, they were invited to the Association of Finnish Travel Agents – AFTA.

2004 they opened an office in Kuopio , which was the company's original rental location in the 1980's. In April 2004, Touring Cars received a special acknowledgement in the Finnish Tourist Board's quality competition. In 2004, they managed to increase sales by 25 %. Lakselv rental station was closed due to a lack of charter flights.

In the beginning of the year 2005 Touring Cars opened a new web-site to serve its international clients. Touring Cars received a quality award from the Finnish Tourist Board for continuous quality improvements and high quality standards. In September 2005, the Finnish travel industry selected Touring Cars as the most innovative tourism company in Finland. In 2003, 2004 and 2005 Touring Cars Finland Oy received a triple A credit score from Dunn and Bradstreet. The now belonged to the top 3,7 % of all corporations in Finland based on this credit score.

In 2006, the company has 125 mobile homes for hire. Solifer and Hymer are the manufacturing partners. The four Finnish rental stations represent 50 % of the operations; the other half comes from Stockholm and Oslo stations. Nevertheless, only less than 10 % of the customers are Finnish. About 800 families per year use the services, spending about 9000 nights in Nordic countries and the Baltics. This means about 30.000 overnights. The challenge is to lengthen the season by offering new products heading to southern parts of Europe. 120 tour-operators sell the services all over the world. The variety of products consists of packaged tours, traditional rentals and several kind of special products. The campers are well equipped and of high quality.

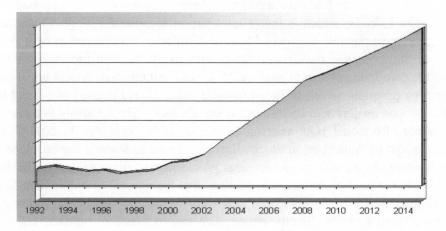

Figure 1: Sales growth up to 2006 and sales forcast up to 2014
(Source: Touring Cars Finland Ltd)

3   Case Analysis

The development of this small but fast growing family enterprise shows that the role of innovativeness of the entrepreneur herself is the key success factor of the company. The characteristics typical of a successful entrepreneur are the ability to take risks, innovativeness, knowledge of how markets function, manufacturing know-how, marketing skills, business management skills and the ability to co-operate. (e.g. Littunen 2000, 295)

Individual innovation is a rich and elusive construct that has been defined and operationalized differently by various researchers. Generally, the construct has been conceptualized in terms of individual characteristics, traits, behaviours and products. According to Drucker (1985) creativity, imagination and generally open attitude toward change contribute to create an innovative environment. Factors relating to individual creativity include personality, attitudes, ability, cognition and motivation. Openness to experience is a personality trait associated with individual creative performance in organizations. Divergent thinking, the process of generating many and differing ideas, is an important aspect of individual creativity in organizations. (Williams 2004) It is evident that Tanja's creativity and ability to solve practical problems with the help of divergent thinking, was in the beginning of the story of this company the decisive ability to survive. Her ability to take controllable risks and the patience to build a long term plan to organise the operations, were also skills that guaranteed the survival in the beginning and the growth over time.

To be an innovative company calls for innovative behaviour. Kleysen and Street (2001) defined innovative behaviour as all individual actions directed at the generation, introduction and/or application of beneficial novelty at any organizational level. Such beneficial novelty might include the development of new product ideas or technologies, changes in administrative procedures aimed at improving work relations or the application of new ideas or technologies to work processes intended to significantly enhance their efficiency and effectiveness. Based on an extensive literature review they recognised five factors seeming best to categorize behaviours associated with individual innovation: opportunity exploration, generativity, formative investigation, championing and application. (Kleysen et al 2001, 285)

Opportunity exploration relates to the metaphor of travelling extensively through innovation opportunities in order to learn or discover more about them. Four basic behaviours concerning opportunity exploration include paying attention to opportunity sources, looking for opportunities to innovate, recognizing opportunities and gathering information about opportunities. (Kleysen et al 2001, 285). The TCF case shows several examples of Tanja's exceptional ability to realise opportunities in the environment. E.g. Tanja's mother's former experience and relationships in retailing businesses were crucial in 1990' when the company was still operating in the Russian market. The notion to combine travel businesses with retailing in these early operations gave the company opportunities to do profitable businesses.

Formative investigation is concerned with giving form to and flushing out ideas, solutions, and opinions and trying them out through investigation. (Kleysen et al 2001, 286) During the latest years the company has been innovative in inverting the potential costs as profits. The company tends to be very practical and profit oriented in their operations. Most of the new service ideas are rooted from a need to solve a practical problem concerning the implementation of an actual service process: when there is a need to transfer vehicles from Finland to Sweden and Norway in the early summer season, the practical problem is how to do it with a minimum cost. By launching the Legoland package for Finnish customers the transfer cost turned to a new product: Rent the camper in Finland, ferry trip to Stockholm, visit to Legoland in Denmark, return the camper in Stockholm, back to Finland by a ferry (http://www.touringcars.fi).

Generativity deals with behaviours directed at generating beneficial change for the purpose of "growing" organizations, their people, products, processes and services. Generativity entails three basic behaviours, including generating ideas and solutions to opportunities, generating representations and categories of opportunities and generating associations and combinations of ideas and information. (Kleysen et al 2001, 286). When Tanja was asked, what the key to their success and rapid growth is, the answer was clear: they have managed to build a great team with complementary capabilities, which makes the company strong and innovative. As their core competence she announced the ability "to have fun", meaning that the work has to be enjoyable for everybody in the team. Tanja herself and Tom, the operational manager, form the innovation team, and other member of the staff take care of the operative implementation of the businesses. According to Tanja there is a rule that she and Tom, use 20 % of their time in routines and 80 % is reserved for being "creative lunatics". The company has out-sourced most of the operative processes and the staff concentrates in marketing, sales and quality control.

Championing consists of the socio-political behaviours involved in processes of innovation, which are essential to realizing the potential of ideas, solutions, and innovations. Individuals that create ideas are able to mobilise resources, persuade and influence other people, push and negotiate their opinions and are ready to take risks and challenges to reach their objectives.

(Kleysen et al 2001, 286-287) All these abilities and characteristics are emphasised in Tanja's personality and in her team.

Application involves working at making innovations a regular part of business as usual. Three basic behaviours regarding application are found commonly throughout the literature including: implementing, modifying and routinizing. (Kleysen et al 2001, 285- 287) This indicates that the company has been very active in developing the innovative environment of the growing company by providing the employees with the best technical facilities, organising the internal information flow and developing their service processes with the camper owner network. One of the most important factors is an understanding of the importance of a workable quality system.

4   Conclusion

Although the innovativeness and creativeness of the entrepreneur herself has shown to be the foundation of the success of the company, the team around her has been crucial. According to Mikki, Tanja's creativity is incessant, but her patience to work the idea till the practical end is not sufficient to realise all the ideas. The team is a kind of controller, which then assesses the ideas, and plans the implementation. This case study supports Zhao's (2005) integrated framework for innovation and entrepreneurship. The framework involves the "5Ss" of strategy, system, staff, skills and style.

A well-defined and pro-active strategy is central to an innovative and entrepreneurial organisation. The control and management system for R&D and new product development should be flexible – depending on the changing situational conditions affecting each project or program. Staff members in an innovative and entrepreneurial organisation must be creative people with a flair for innovation. Clearly, an innovative and entrepreneurial organisation needs a range of managerial and entrepreneurial capacities and skills to handle innovation. (Zhao 2005) Innovation capacity can be proposed as a high-order integration capability, that is, an ability to mould and manage multiple capabilities (Lawson & Samson 2001). Ilomäki et al. (2005) use the term innovation capability, which is an ability to continuously transform knowledge and ideas to new products, processes and systems for the benefit of the company and its stakeholders.

Additionally, an ideal entrepreneurial management style for innovation should be open and supportive, should encourage and nurture new product development. The style of an innovative and entrepreneurial organisation should provide employees with a culture of empowerment and should boast a reward system that provides incentives for innovative and entrepreneurial behaviours, values, and assumptions (Zhao 2005).

References

Drucker, P. (1985), Innovation and Entrepreneurship, New York: Harper Business.

Dömötör, R. & Hader, C. (2005), Traits vs. Attitudes as Measures for the Prediction of Entrepreneurship, in: RENT XIX – Research on Entrepreneurship and Small Business, Entrepreneurship, Competitiveness and Local Development, Naples (Italy), 16–18 November 2005, CD-ROM publication, pp. 1–13.

Ilomäki, S-K., Koivisto, T., Airola, M. & Poikkimäki, J. (2005), A theoretical approach to strategic innovation capability in SMEs, in: RENT XIX – Research on Entrepreneurship and Small Business, Entrepreneurship, Competitiveness and Local Development, Naples (Italy), 16–18 November 2005, CD-ROM publication, pp. 1–8.

Kleysen, R. F. & Street, C. T. (2001), Toward a multi-dimensional measure of individual innovative behaviour, in: Journal of Intellectual Capital, Vol. 2, No. 3, pp. 284–296.

Littunen, H. (2000), Entrepreneurship and the characteristics of the entrepreneurial personality, in: International Journal of Entrepreneurial Behavior & Research, Vol 6, No. 6, pp. 295–309.

Williams, S. D. (2004), Personality, attitude, and leader influences on divergent thinking and creativity in organizations, European Journal of Innovation Management, Vol. 7, No. 3, pp. 187–204.

Zhao, F. (2005), Exploring the synergy between entrepreneurship and innovation, in: International Journal of Entrepreneurial Behaviour & Research, Vol. 11, No. 1, pp. 25–41.

FRANCOIS VELLAS AND VALÉRIE BRIVE

The Case of Transmontagne

1 Presentation of Transmontagne

Transmontagne is a group located in Villeurbanne, a town in the suburb of Lyon. It is the third French group and is primarily a manager of ski-lifts. It has as it's ambition to become the European leader for the management of intermediate ski stations. There are approximately 200 intermediate ski stations throughout Europe.

2 The Missions of Transmontagne

Transmontagne organises and maintains the skiing business, produces artificial snow, provides security on the slopes, and is responsible for the exploitation and the maintenance of the ski- lifts. Furthermore, the group runs and develops tourist places. It is a specialist for the maintenance, the exploitation, and the development of ski stations. Since 2000, it has decided to diversify these activities and wanted to promote other leisure activities and sports. The group also offers its technical support to the organizers of special events and operations. In addition to all these actions, Transmontagne invests in different fields in order to generate more income. Currently, this group is expanding rapidly. It's notable why its investments must be maintained and reinforced.

Financing of activities: Philippe Gausset, founder of Transmontagne created a holding named "Montagnes Finances". He is now the first stakeholder of this holding. CDC Services and Enterprises also participate with 30 %. CDC Services Industries invests in European and French companies, usually companies which are not on stock exchange and with a turnover between EUR 15 and 120 millions. CDC Services Industrie invests in every field of industry and services, except in high technology industries.

Objectives of Transmontagne: The group tries to increase the volume of the natural heritage, to optimise the development of the economic activities, of employment and training. Philippe Gausset develops a long-term strategy for his company.

The priority is the quality of the services provided by the group. Therefore, the focus is on a better reception of guests, on the security for customers and employees (especially when they are on the ski- lifts), and on the provision of secured slopes. Another goal is to "integrate" carefully all their activities in the natural environment of mountains. Philippe Gausset says that it's really important to respect the natural landscapes and to have adapted constructions. This is why he developed a program for the preservation of the environment.

Transmontagne is responsible for many accommodations throughout France and manages "Transmontagne Résidences" which aims to deal with the residences and the reception of guests on site, the door-to-door selling of new customers, and the development of relationships with other partners, in order to have better and more competitive prices than its competitors. Moreover, Transmontagne wants to search for new investments. Since 2005, the group has evoked a new goal which is to balance the tourism season in the ski resorts, and to lengthen the duration of tourism there. The group also focused on ski resorts which have to deal with a global problem: during the winter, they are a famous vacation places for well-off people, but during the summer, they don't attract many tourists. They are not perceived as real sites of leisure activities and people prefer to spend their holidays on the country sides rather than coming to mountains. The slogan of the group is: "Transmontagne, for a controlled management".

3   History of Transmontagne

1991	Creation of the group, and first contract of ski lifts with the ski station of Valfréjus
1992	Development of the activity of accommodation in Valfréjus
1993	One contract with Lioran and another one with Praloup (ski lifts)
1996	Contract with La Tania about accommodation and, contract for the concession of the "Funicular of the Pic du Jer"
1998	Contract of buying of Chamrousse an dits ski lifts
1999	Contract of buying of Dévoluy (ski lifts and accommodation)
2002	Transformation of the contracts of Valfréjus and Praloup into contracts of concession and contract with Cap Découverte (sports and fun)
2003	New organisation of the group; Contract which created Ski Dubai in the United Arab Emirates
2004	Contract of buying of Bardonnecchia, in Italy (ski lifts). In addition to this, Transmontagne became manager of Le Queyras (ski lifts). Then, contract of buying of Kanin Bovec, in Slovenia (ski lifts)
2005	Creation of the "Alpvision Développement Society" in Switzerland, and buying of shares of Télénendaz (Valais suisse)
2006	Management of a new residence in Nendaz, Pracondu, Switzerland, and creation of the "Transalpina Sviluppo Society", Italy

Some data about Transmontagne: Currently, Transmontagne manages:

- 188 ski- lifts.
- 645 slopes.
- 597 snow canons.
- 55 snow cats
- 300 permanent employees
- 1710 seasonal employees

In 2005, the turnover reached EUR 43 million. 70 % of the turnover (equivalent to EUR 31.8 million) is realised by the exploitation of tourist sites and ski stations. The accommodation represents 22 % of the turnover. 6 % of it comes from the renting of skis, and 3 % from food and beverage activities.

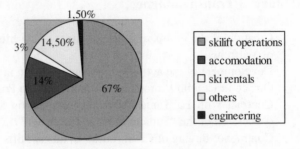

Figure 1: Allocation of turnover

The president and his teams: professionals attending the customers: Philippe Gausset is the founder of Transmontagne. He insists on having a management which is close to customers' needs and he gathered around him a big team of moutain specialists, for the reception, sale, and maintenance of the slopes and built constructions. Every tourist site is directly managed by a local president who is responsible for the dialogue between all the partners of the area. There are 2 key ideas mission objectives: professionalisation and training. Transmontagne is vary attentive to the professionalisation of its teams. This is why it proposes education and training courses for all employees who are willing to improve their skills. The training is really useful, especially nowadays with a working population who is becoming older. Philippe Gausset is aware of the necessity to replace them by younger ones which from now on have to be trained.

In addition to this, Transmontagne developed different programs and continuous efforts in order to associate the seasonal workers to the organisational culture of the enterprise. The enterprise wants to have more and more sustainable jobs in its different departments. According to the various seasons throughout the year, Transmontagne proposes to seasonal workers, some additional activities on the tourist sites. In this perspective, the group created "Transmontagne Maintenance" which illustrates the desire to struggle against precarious work of its employees. The enterprise is going to employ about 100 people during the low season in order to maintain the ski lifts and all of the tourist residences. Until now, both activities have always been subcontracted, for an amount of EUR 1.2 million.

4 Functional and Legal Organisation of Transmontagne

The organisation of Transmontagne is articulated around 5 poles:

- ski resorts
- management of accommodations
- tourist sites for the summer period (Transmontagne Residences)
- renting and sale of ski equipments (Ski Pro)
- transport and engineering for mountainous regions (TIM)

In order to help the group in its daily job, Transmontagne works in collaboration with local partners (such as community councils, regional governance, tourism boards, ski schools, sport clubs, shops…), and supports different initiatives aimed at improving the relationship with customers.

Professionals who are recognized and requested worldwide: Transmontagne selects residences and accommodations which suit different criteria which have been enacted by the executives of the enterprise, namely: the beauty of the landscapes, the comfort of the flats, the diversity and originality of the services proposed. All of these criteria are seen as a guarantee of a high quality service.

Due to its past experiences and its knowledge, Transmontagne is nowadays also asked to manage other tourist activities (and not exclusively ski stations), such as:

- CAP DECOUVERTE, Tarn, France: Cap Decouverte proposes a wide range of leisure and entertainment activities in an old quarry.
- FUNICULAR of PIC du JER, in the Pyrénées: This cable car is a famous tourists' attraction throughout the urban area, and takes all its passengers from the valley up to the highest point of Lourdes.

Development of additional services: As all its activities are gathered around the same destinations, Transmontagne developed some "all inclusive" packages (with ski pass, accommodation, renting or sale of equipments…).

In order to maintain a wide range of activities for customers through the ski station, Transmontagne decided to develop Ski Pro, which is the manager of rental and sales of ski equipments on different sites. Via its subsidiary TIM (Transport and Engineering in Mountains), Transmontagne proposes advice and assistance throughout the ski season for regions and towns. For instance, TIM gives advices for the building and the modernisation of systems of transport with ski-lifts, funicular, trains and cable cars.

Furthermore, TIM proposes opportunities of developing entertainment spaces and ski lifts. To sum up, TIM has developed over 150 projects and worked in partnership the major projects of Transmontagne in France and abroad.

The activity of management in ski resorts (and initiatives): In France, the group of companies is at the present time in every mountainous region. Thus, Transmontagne manages the ski stations (and the ski- lifts) of Chamrousse (Isère), Valfréjus (Savoie), Super Dévoluy (Hautes- Alpes), Pra- Loup (Alpes de Haute Provence) and Lioran (Cantal). It is also responsible for shops of renting skis in Super Dévoluy and Valfréjus, and supervises mountain restaurants in Valfréjus, Super Dévoluy, Lioran, Carmaux and Pic du Jer. In addition to that, it has a major role in the management of the nautical base of Garabit (Cantal), the site of Pic du Jer (especially during the summer), and the entertainment base of Cap Decouverte (Tarn). Moreover, the group has just invested EUR 3.5 millions in order to inaugurate a new (4 seats) chair-lift in Valfréjus. It now connects the ski station to the plateau of Arronda. Besides, the group bought five ski shops in Valfréjus, which reinforces its position in this domain of activity and which, until now, was developed only in Super Dévoluy.

The Example of Chamrousse: This ski station used to be a gathering of buildings occupied by French winter campers only. These have been transformed into small chalets 3* with all the comfort expected by customers. This transformation has been the biggest project of rehabilitation in mountains in France. And Transmontagne built new ski lifts in order to link the new chalets and the slopes. The town did not have any extra cost, and all of the investments were done by Transmontagne. The group is also responsible for the marketing of its tourist products to tour operators. It has been a huge success: all accommodations have been booked only two months after the inauguration and the ski stations are working at full capacity. Chamrousse is a beautiful example of development for ski stations in middle-high mountains (intermediate mountains)!

Management activities in the field of accommodations: Even though the core strategy of Transmontagne is based on the activity of management of ski stations (and ski lifts), the management of tourist residences is becoming increasingly important. Here a new tendency towards consumerism can be observed: nowadays, people don't go to ski stations only for skiing: the entertainment criterion is essential to attracting more and more tourists. That's why new residences are no longer built at the bottom of ski slopes: because skiing is only but one activity (among others) in the resort. Thus, in Central Europe, accommodations can be located quite far away from the slopes. The latter doesn't bother customers as long as the residences are modern, comfortable and fully equipped. Nowadays, Transmontagne tries to attract a new category of customers and builds SPA and fitness rooms in the residences. Thus the level of services has become quite high.

However, for this activity, Transmontagne has many competitors such as Immo Investir, MGM, Lagrange Patrimoine Conseil or Pierre & Vacances Conseil Immobilier. All of these French companies try to have an increasing number of services in order to attract new customers. This is why competition to attract customers (and more important, to create a sort of fidelity) has become really hard!

The demand of accommodation is also increasing rapidly and customers are searching for professionals who can adapt the products to their needs at a reasonable price.

Number of managed flats by Transmontagne:

- Chamrousse: 616
- La Joue du Loup: 107
- Le Queyras: 81
- Puy St Vincent: 217
- Super Dévoluy: 409
- Termignon la Vanoise: 193
- Valfréjus: 463
- Bardonecchia (Italie): 124
- Nendaz (Valais Suisse): 36

To sum up, we can notice that Transmontagne manages a total of 2246 flats during the winter of 2006/2007.

The strategy of Transmontagne: a persisting presence in France and new International targets: In 2004, in addition to the rehabilitation of the Bachat-Bouloud site, near Chamrousse, Transmontagne invested EUR 20 millions in new chair- lifts and ski- lifts. The group always makes new investments in order to be modern and competitive. The strategy focus of P. Gausset was to cover all over France from the beginning. But, he realized that he had to be more aggressive on the international market and, in April 2004, faced his first challenge abroad. Philippe Gausset bought the Italian ski station of Bardonecchia. Today, he controls 98.2 % of the equity of this cable car company. Following this, Transmontagne worked in order to develop its activities throughout the world, and created, in Slovenia, a firm called Transkanin Doo (Philippe Gausset owns 80 % of the capital) which manages a ski domain consisting of 30 kilometres of slopes (an area which will double during the 2 next years). Moreover in Italy, the group bought the Sella Nevea ski station, and will develop a link between the Italian ski domain and the Slovenian one.

Despite all of these acquisitions, Philippe Gausset still focuses on its primary strategy of being present only in the intermediate mountains.

5   Conclusion on Future Perspectives

Besides being a competitive group, always searching for new markets and targets, Transmontagne has a powerful team and a president who is innovative and isn't afraid of challenge. He develops a unique ambition which aims to maintain the core strategy (ski-lifts), but continues to increase the management of tourist residences in France, and to diversify its activities throughout the world. The group enacts ambitious growing goals for years to come. However, they are totally aware of future tendencies such as the inevitable need of linking the European ski stations. Increasing competition and the operation cost of all its properties. Transmontagne has many driving forces and is very flexible: it can rapidly adjust to new customers' demands and needs. Its growth is becoming more and more important. Mountain regions will afford attractive perspectives for Transmontagne for years to come.

Harald Pechlaner and Elisabeth Fischer

JOSKA Kristall – Leading Tourist Company and World Market Leader in the Glass Manufacturing Industry

1   Introduction

Different globalization trends in the tourism industry generate high dynamic forces in terms of competition. The rules of competition and industry standards are constantly changing. Innovative companies are challenged to act and react quickly and systematically in order to keep up with the competitors. Especially small and medium-sized enterprises, which mark the tourism sector, often have only limited resources available. As far as innovative companies on the market are concerned, it can be noticed that more and more originally non-tourist companies and service providers enter the field of tourism. Often companies that have transferred their services to a new sector offer top quality level in the new sector, surpassing the traditional players of the sector itself, and in many cases becoming leading companies.

This case represents the thesis that innovations result from specific entrepreneurial competencies and finally the transfer of products and services to other sectors and new markets. In the tourism industry it is often necessary to overcome the obstacles of scarce resources in small and medium-sized enterprises in terms of the development of innovations. Thus, a standardized innovation process is hardly possible; innovations must be generated in accordance with the company's structure to produce best possible quality.

This article shows the example of the company JOSKA Kristall GmbH & Co KG, a medium-sized glass manufacturing company in the Bavarian Forest, and a family business in their second generation. The business was started in the 1960s as a mere glass manufacturing company. Today, it is the world market leader in producing glass trophies as well as a leading tourist company of the region. With the construction of an innovative world of experience, the owner of the company has transferred the business of glassware to the tourism industry. He constantly develops appropriate new tourist concepts. The company knows how to profit from the synergies of both sectors in order to develop competitive advantages in each business area. With the example of JOSKA Kristall, the driving powers and success factors of innovative medium-sized enterprises in the tourism industry can be demonstrated. But first, the term innovation will be defined in the following section, and subsequently the innovation processes in general as well as the situation of innovations in the tourism industry will be described.

2   Innovations in the Tourism Industry

The literature shows many different definitions of the term innovation (for an overview see Hausschildt 1993, p. 5). For Hausschildt (1993) innovations are qualitative innovative products or methods which clearly differ from their previous form. However, it is a precondition that an innovation is realized and understood. Innovation can mean that purposes and means are combined in as yet unknown form which must stand up in the market or business use. In the tourism sector, innovators face aggravated conditions due to the nature of the product and the structure of the sector (Pechlaner et al. 2006a). On the one hand, the industry's structure is marked by small and medium-sized enterprises, and on the other hand, innovations of services and experiences often face the problem that the process of diffusion starts very quickly, i.e. innovations are imitated very quickly. Compared with material goods, innovations can hardly be protected by patents, and thus they nearly have the nature of a public good. Consequently, the innovator has to struggle with non-internalizable positive external effects of innovation as well as free-riders (Pechlaner et al. 2006a, Tschurtschenthaler 2005).

Innovations require venture as well as equity capital. Small and medium-sized enterprises lack time, money and know-how to manage the amount of information and to work out an operationalizable form or a standardized innovation process, like it is possible in big companies. Thus, innovation capacity correlates with the size of the enterprise (Rogers 1983, Dosi 1988). For small and medium-sized enterprises it is often not profitable to invest in a standardized concept development and in innovations; therefore, they rather chose the strategy of imitation. But in order to stay competitive and to offer valuable and attractive offers, it is also very important for small and medium-sized enterprises in the tourism industry to offer high-quality products demanded by the market constantly. Hence, this case posits the thesis that also small and medium-sized enterprises can create innovations by regular quality management and high-quality offers. Innovative concepts and products result from the strategy of quality leadership and the entrepreneurial ability to transfer competencies to or from (a) new market(s). Tourism of quality can also mean innovative tourism for a company.

First, the case describes competencies that mark high-quality tourism. Quality in the tourism industry requires professional control of the business processes, certain accessibility to the customer, marketability, a coherent concept, professional marketing, and the regionalization of competencies:

- A basic requirement for service-providers of adventures and experience is to cope with the process flow of the company in order to make the companies generally competitive in the market place.

- When it comes to services, production and consumption happen at the same time. Due to the so-called uno-acto principle (Bieger 2002), the accessibility to the customer is part of the core business in tourism. Hospitality is an important criterion of quality. The necessary frankness and accessibility to the customer is on the one hand essential to the tourist entrepreneur, on the other hand it serves to enhance the service according to demand.

- Only if all elements of the service portfolio are harmoniously combined with the business concept, is it authentic for the guest. In this context, architecture, communicated issues, the range of products, the outward presentation of services and the company, the appearance of the personnel etc. play an important role. Authenticity can be compared with honesty.

- Professional target-group-oriented advertising and communication guarantee that the "right" guest is invited directly by the company and that the right expectations are met. This is a key factor for the satisfaction of the guests and for the atmosphere of the site of attraction.

- A minimum of network measures are necessary for the tourist entrepreneur due to the nature of the destination product. Cooperation with providers of regional complementary products, e.g. regional suppliers, regional products or service personnel from the region, increase the authentic effect of the offer; thus, they can hardly be imitated because of their regional specification (Pechlaner/Fischer 2006). Moreover, synergies and better conditions by regional cooperation and at best a common development of competencies can be archived. The regionalization of competencies is thus not only the deciding factor for the quality improvement of the service offer but it can also present an important protection against imitation and facilitate early reactions to environmental changes. In this context, the formation of clusters and districts play an important role.

The competencies that are necessary for a high-quality tourism product can also be interesting for other markets in order to establish new business opportunities. The entrepreneur must know how to recognize, develop and transfer these competencies (Prahalad/Hamel 1990). Innovations can be generated by small and medium-sized enterprises if they feature the entrepreneurial know-how to transport competencies, ideas, concepts, issues or products from or into other sectors. On the one hand, competencies and ideas can be transferred from other sectors to their own markets and thus constitute something new. On the other hand, new markets can be opened within their own sectors or in entirely new industries with company-owned core competencies. Due to the fact that company-specific competencies are transferred, the life cycle of products can be extended, the competency can be enhanced by new experiences, and costs can be saved by the use of synergies. In order to transfer competencies, the company must be aware of its core competencies. Core competencies form the basis in the innovation process (Pechlaner et al. 2005a, Pechlaner/Fischer 2006). Based on that, issues, concepts and technologies can be transferred to new markets, both within the sector and also in new sectors (Pechlaner et. al. 2005b).

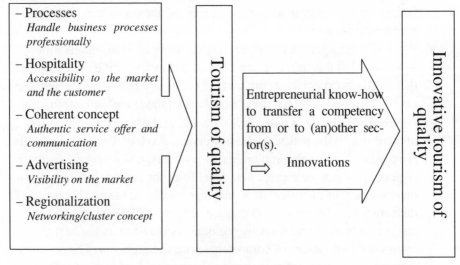

Figure 1: Connection between Tourism of quality and Innovative tourism,
(Source: Own illustration)

One example for a company creating innovations with its products and issues in other sectors is the concept of the industrial world of experience illustrated in the following example of JOSKA Kristall: An industrial company transfers its products and industry domain business to the leisure and tourism industry (Hinterhuber/ Pechlaner 2001, Pechlaner et al. 2006b). With the transfer to the leisure industry, the company is confronted with a new competitive environment including the specific characteristics of the tourism industry. The industrial site becomes a point of attraction; there is a metamorphosis where the customer is also a guest and the entrepreneur is a host and entertainer: "A good industrial world of experience must meet the following requirements: be authentic like a good museum, feature didactic qualities like a BBC documentary, be entertaining like a leisure park and customer-friendly like an Austrian family hotel" (Steiner in Pechlaner et al. 2006b, p. 89). These are the competencies that the producer of material goods must know if he starts to produce emotions and services. Compared to material goods, experiences and services are immaterial, high-integrative products. They involve new management tasks and competence requirements which represents a big challenge for an industrial company as it has to overcome some barriers and obstacles (Pechlaner et al. 2006b). However, this can constitute a big potential for innovations for a company. In the following case, the example of the glass manufacturing company JOSKA Kristall[2] is developed; the company has successfully transferred the issue of glassware to the tourism industry, and it has already become a leading tourist company. At the same time, the medium-sized enterprise is world market leader in the production and the design of glass trophies for big sports events. The owner of the company knows well how to combine the synergies and the innovative potential of both sectors in order to use the development of competitive advantages in both business branches which is what makes the medium-sized enterprise in the middle of the Bavarian Forest to an innovative and world-wide successful company.

---

[2] Within the scope of an analysis of the winners of the Award of Innovation for innovative tourist offers, which is awarded by BAYERN TOURISMUS Marketing GmbH in Bavaria in different categories every year, of the last five years (2002-2006), JOSKA Kristall was awarded the most innovative company according to the criteria of Innovative Entrepreneurial Network (EIN) of AIEST.

3   The Case JOSKA Kristall GmbH & Co KG[3]

The company: The glass manufacturing company JOSKA Kristall GmbH & Co KG is a medium-sized family-business in its second generation. The company's production site is situated in Bodenmais in the Bavarian Forest where a 70,000 square-meter world of experience was established, which demonstrates the company's variety of imaginativeness. The products range from exclusive wine glassware to candleholders or crystal chandeliers, all are a show case of the company's creativity. The crystalline world combines the competencies of the company, from the creativity of the design studio, glass-blowers and grinders to service-orientation. The crystal universe attracts more than one million visitors every year. Today, the company JOSKA Kristall has about 230 employees and it is the world market leader in producing glass trophies, and a leading tourist company of the region. In 2004, the enterprise was awarded the price of innovation for its arrangement of product and service offers by BAYERN TOURISMUS Marketing GmbH in the category "family holidays" for the innovative tourism product "glass experience weeks".

Cornerstones of the company

1960 Formation of the glass-processing company

1975 Construction of an additional forest glasswork built according to historical plans.

1990 Joining the trophy business

1993 Construction of the world of experience

2003 Takeover of management by Josef Kagerbauer Jr.

2004 Award of Innovation by Bayern Tourismus Marketing GmbH for "glass experience weeks"

2006 The company has approx. 230 employees

Figure 2: Cornerstones of the company

---

[3]   The following specifications are based on the results of a qualitative interview with the entrepreneur Josef Kagerbauer Jr. carried out on July 14, 2006, as well as a report in the journal Vivre July/August 2006

In the following section, the company and its history will be decribes. The developments will be presents and then the driving forces and success factors for the development of the innovations will be analyzed.

The background: The company is situated in Bodenmais in the Bavarian Forest. Bavaria is the province with the largest number of overnight stays in the Federal Republic of Germany[4.] In the Bavarian Forest glass manufacturing features a 700-year old tradition. The "Glass Route", a tourist theme route in the Bavarian Forest region, also leads through Bodenmais.

46 years ago, Josef Kagerbauer Sr. founded the glass manufacturing enterprise together with his wife Georgine. Today, Josef Kagerbauer Jr. runs the company. He has studied the glass handcraft in every detail and has passed all stations of training starting from glass blowing to special glass manufacturing techniques. In New York he was taught the art of glass by famous Stuart Abelmann. However, at the age of 24, Josef Kagerbauer Jr. decided to work in the sports sector and developed a BodyFit fitness concept presented in Munich, North Rhine-Westphalia, and the United States. At that time, he made important contacts with national and international top athletes; it turned out that these contacts would be very helpful for his later business. Finally, at the age of 30, he returned to Bodenmais to work in the family business where he realized the idea of the "world of experience".

The success story: The company has now been in business for two generations. When Josef Kagerbauer Sr. founded the enterprise, it was a mere handcraft business. However, tourism had already been linked with the business at the beginning of the formation of the company. Compared to the other glassworks in the Bavarian-Bohemian Forest, already at that time Josef Kagerbauer Sr. followed an offensive strategy by welcoming guests to the Bavarian Forest showing them the secrets of his handcraft. The company was the first glasswork ever that allowed tourists to take a look behind the scenes, and thus the company became a famous point of attraction in the region. In the 1980s, the company actively started to present itself at tourism fairs. In the 1990s, traditional Bavarian-Bohemian glassware started to decline but Josef Kagerbauer succeeded in opening a new market with the production of glass trophies and thus transferred the core competence of the company, i.e.

---

4   cf. Bavarian Ministry of State for Economy, Infrastructure, Traffic and Technology: Tourism in Bavaria, June 2005, p. 2: According to the Federal Government Statistics in 2004, compared with other federal states, Bavaria holds the leading position with almost 74 million overnight stays (accommodation providers with 9 guest beds and more, as well as campsites) of a total of approx. 340 million overnight stays in Germany, followed by Baden-Württemberg (40.0 million), North Rhine-Westphalia (37.7 million) and Lower Saxony (34.5 million).

glass manufacturing by grinding, to a new product. Today, JOSKA Kristall is a world market leader in this sector. The businessman realized very early that glassware is an exchangeable product and that exclusivity is created by outside design, marketing as well as emotional experience. When the company headquarters in Bodenmais became too small, the idea of the "world of experience" in the neighbourhood was designed where Josef Kagerbauer Jr. was inspired by his experiences in the US. From the very beginning, he was convinced that the American strategy of adventure shopping would also be successful in Germany. With technical presentations and the "look and feel" concept, emotions are to be stimulated which the customers combine with glassware and finally with the company. The company offers a wide range of experiences for tourists. The concept also aims at welcoming children who are attracted by the product and thus becoming attached to the company.

For the glass experience weeks, invented in 2003, the company was awarded the price of innovation by Bayern Tourismus Marketing GmbH. Children and adults are entertained in the crystal world of experience; they can paint on glass, learn how to blow glass or make engravings. The product is offered as a package with different elements. On account of the popularity of those service packages, there are also glass experience days, and also other service offers and attractions along the glass route. However, the company differs from its competitors with its wide range of offers and especially with the crystal world of experience. Thus, the innovative idea to work together with tourists to gain the acceptability of the customers and to get them interested in the product was already initiated by the founder of the company; today his son continues this strategy by innovative and very professional developments.

The tourism industry in the Bavarian Forest has constantly been rising, a good hotel infrastructure has been developed, and the company JOSKA has always been oriented by tourism which has contributed to its development and new orientation. Today, the tourist attraction features a leading position in the region. Mr. Kagerbauer sees himself as a tourism expert. With always new ideas and events, he attracts new segments of visitors to the world of experience. According to the principle "Magic and Seduction", visitors are first attracted by the handcraft and then by the product.

Today's success of the company JOSKA Kristall is therefore based on two essential product innovations which the owner of the company has created during the last ten years: first, the world of experience with the concept of adventure shopping and the emotionalization of glassware which has become a popular tourist attraction, and second, the glass trophy which enabled the company to conquer the world market and to replace the metal cup. Together with this renovation, the new technique of laser engraving was developed. The creation of both innovations was made possible by the company's transfer of one competence to a new market.

Innovation No. 1: Emotionalization of glassware – the world of glass experience. When the production site in the village became too small, and Bodenmais was turned into a climatic health resort, a solution to the traffic situation due to the many visitors of JOSKA was needed. Therefore, an idea was realized to resettle some parts of the company, which was the starting signal for the implementation of a new innovative concept – the world of glass experience.

Another motive for the basic idea of the development and implementation of the world of experience was that the glass industry had been changing since the foundation of the company. The once popular Bohemian Forest glassware had disappeared from the market. In the 1990s, competitors achieved a production innovation with simple elegant undecorated glass; thus, a new trend was set which replaced ground glass. Ground products once made up 90 per cent of the product range of JOSKA Kristall as the company's production was started with these products. With the new trend the product became comparable and had no unique selling proposition anymore which decisively contributed to the development of a new concept. Joska's new strategy was called "look and feel". Unique selling proposition was developed with design, with lasting experience oriented by the tourism industry. Guests are potential customers and the product has even become a product of a generation. Families make holidays in the Bavarian Forest because their children like to stay there.

Tourism got a new role in the strategic perspective of the company. Since its foundation, the company's sales idea had been the main focus in terms of synergetic use of tourism. But then the experience and emotionalization of the product turned it into a strategy of differentiation. Thus, experience has become the unique selling proposition. Glassware is interchangeable, but linked with JOSKA's experience it becomes unique and not imitable. The company's innovation is its presentation in a world of experience. JOSKA has recognized that successful management of a world of experience is only possible with innovative products which are attractive for the tourism industry and its market.

It is important to emotionalize people and to make a link to glassware. As the company's strategy was initially only focused on handcraft, it has now expanded to more tourist dimensions. Tourism is now seen as a connection to the market.

Innovation No. 2: World-famous glass trophies: Following the new trend of elegantly non-ground glassware, JOSKA faced the problem that a new utilization had to be found for the existing competencies of glass grinding in the company. With the trophies, JOSKA filled a gap in the market and found a new product for the technique of glass grinding. The contacts to the sports business and the specification in glass grinding featured resources which were combined and adopted. Thus, the first glass trophies were produced. And finally, also this product has been enhanced; today, the simple glass trophy is a classy trophy. The company is constantly making efforts to enhance the production and process engineering. Thus, together with a company in Los Angeles, JOSKA developed a new process technique for sandblast engravings which enables the enterprise to engrave for example special sponsor logos on glass. The technique is an innovation and therefore represents an important competitive advantage. The glass grinding, glass blowing, and sandblast graving techniques together with the know-how and the sense of design and form of glass which make it possible to design and create a perfect individual trophy for every purpose enabled the company's breakthrough into the sports business. The filigree and innovative artworks have replaced the metal trophies and cups. Today, JOSKA Kristall is a world market leader in this segment. With its trophies, JOSKA Kristall not only marks the sports world – e.g. the company invented the World Cup crystal globe trophy for the best skier – but also famous companies like Lufthansa, Adidas, Mercedes, Microsoft, Siemens, and BMW as well as very important people from the sports business, from society and politics have become loyal customers of crystal trophies, i.e. the crystal world in Bodenmais has not only become a center of attraction for sports fans but also the birthplace of famous trophies.

The company's core competence could successfully be transferred to a new market and another sector. Synergies with the tourism industry and synergies with the world of experience were found. The visitors are very impressed by the in-house exhibition showing the highlights of the cups and trophies. Being a center of attraction of sports trophies again features a unique selling proposition. The big trophies mark brand recognition that can be found in Bodenmais and can be innovatively combined in the tourism and entertainment sector.

A recipe for success? According to JOSKA, it is important for the identification of a tourist potential to know what people are looking for when they visit the world of experience. To recognize what people want is often very difficult. But in this context, JOSKA works with different concepts: glass experience weeks, the children's land day (kids can search gems), glassblowing, and the family rally. That means concepts which can also be experienced for example with club holidays remodelled for the company JOSKA and the issue of glass. Tourist concepts and competencies have been transferred to the glass handcraft which marks an innovation for a manufacturing company. Here, quality plays a major role for the company and can be demonstrated in the following examination of individual quality competencies.

Hospitality – Accessibility to customers and the market: Originally, Bodenmais was an old mining village. But when mining was stopped, the village became poor because it had no attractions. The founder of the company JOSKA realized very soon that summer visitors coming to the Bavarian Forest, which was at that time still a very rural region without innovations, were potential customers and visitors interested in the handcraft. Being tourist-oriented from the very beginning of its foundation, Mr. Kagerbauer Sr. started to welcome guests and exhibited the art of glass manufacturing. The hen-coop was rebuilt into a showroom, and the guests gave important feedback for the businessman. Today, Mr. Kagerbauer Jr. develops innovative products together with his customers, e.g. a champagne glass without bottom which looks as if a flower was introduced in a vase.

Coherent concept: Enjoying, relaxing, and shopping. The company's philosophy is to provide impulses for action and to communicate the emotions of action to the guest. Entertainment of pleasure and the visualization of action are the slogans of the company. Therefore, one has to be authentic and remain true to the specialization of glassware. This is the motto of Josef Kagerbauer Jr. who always tells his employees: "Show the people what you know. Be proud of what you do and show it." The overall concept is the emotionalization of action.

The principle of "look and feel" had already been applied by the founder of the company. From the very beginning, the concept was perfectly implemented, emotions were awakened and customers were stimulated to buy the products. The strategic elements of the concept are entertainment, catering, shopping, relaxation, and wellness. This idea, being modeled on American entertainment parks, is reflected all over the company, even in the architecture which is uncharacteristic of the Bavarian Forest region but which is nevertheless integrated into the landscape and meets the tourist demands. It is a key factor that the overall concept must be coherent in itself whereas the company is constantly advancing. Next year a big reconstruction measure is planned in the recreational area which is at first not exclusively linked with the sale of glassware but features an overall and coherent tourist concept. The company gets impulses for new innovation activities by mystery shopping and contacts to other tourism experts.

Professional marketing: The owner of the company himself is always surprised how famous his medium-sized enterprise in the Bavarian Forest has become and how many visitors from central Europe are attracted. The first generation assessed the whole idea as industrial selling and profited from the location "Germany". It was the time at the end of the 1970s when "made in Germany" was a seal of quality. However, at that time the company owner actively invited visitors. Bus companies were acquired; print media, flyers and all advertising media available at that time were addressed in order to make the enterprise attractive. Today, professional marketing is very important for the owner of the company. The overall marketing concept is directed to the tourism industry.

Handle processes professionally: For the optimistic entrepreneur who is very keen on sports, quality is essential. Employees are trained by Mr. Kagerbauer and by professional experts who provide motivation trainings. Team spirit and friendliness are very important. JOSKA attaches great importance to authenticity which can very easily be sensed by the customer. Service quality and professionalism are reflected by the employee's friendliness. As far as professionalism is concerned, Mr. Kagerbauer's advice is to remain authentic all the time. The guest recognizes very easily if a product is not authentic, i.e. if it is not lived by the people. A product which is too much styled could be compared with a machine-made product. The company is absolutely aware of its competencies. It is prepared to market glass better than others. It produces experiences. It runs a world of experiences. "We are magicians, seducers", says the owner of the company, and he means "I cannot make a product specific. Maybe that would be professional for the product but not for our action." The competence team that is composed by employees of different departments, from the stocks department to the marketing department, constantly develops the experience schedule where events are planned. The concept is renovated every three years, the event program once a year with thorough consideration of the core competencies and the market. One product is for example the Racing Night, a night ski race that attracts more than 20,000 visitors to Bodenmais.

Regionalization: The entrepreneurial family and the business are strongly rooted in the Bavarian Forest region. The employees come from the neighborhood. Regional integration is also reflected with the suppliers. Orders are only placed to enterprises from Bodenmais and the rural district of Regen. Thus, authenticity is ensured, and the company strengthens its position as a regional leading company. The company works very closely with the municipality of Bodenmais, and the health resort administration department. Already in the 1970s and 80s, they were presented together in tourist fairs. There are cooperation measures with the glass route, the hotels of the region and the national tourism organization.

4   Conclusion

The company's key factor for success is know-how, intention, and motivation. To summarize, the following principles can be derived for innovative companies in the tourism industry. In order to be innovative, companies in the tourism industry must:

- see beyond their businesses.
- react to environmental and competitive changes.
- be willing to be the best.
- remain realistic.
- be enthusiastic about the product and spread enthusiasm.
- challenge and promote employees and stakeholders.

JOSKA sees the product as a medium that transfers the company to the tourism industry. Therefore, the company must know how to fill the people with enthusiasm about what the company does. This is the connection to the market. The owner of the company knows how to combine technology and competency with the market in an innovative manner. As already mentioned in the beginning, it is a challenging task for the entrepreneur to combine technology with the market and to create successful innovations. In this context, the company JOSKA is a perfect example.

Handcraft is still the main focus of the company. However, due to market developments and the change of generations in the company, the tourism aspect has considerably been strengthened in the company strategy and has therefore become very important for the company today. Compared with other comparable worlds of experience, JOSKA has furthermore realized that it is necessary in the tourism industry – even though it represents one business area apart from the main business – to produce high quality. This can only be made possible if that area is appropriately presented in the company strategy. And his success proves to be real. Similar worlds of experience feature 45,000 to 300,000 visitors per year; JOSKA has one million visitors per year. Finally, this innovative strategy turns out to be very profitable.

References

Bieger, T. (2002): Management von Destinationen, Oldenbourg, München und Wien

Dosi, G. (1988): The nature of the innovation process, in: Dosi, G. et al. (eds.): Technical Change and Economic Theory, London, p. 221–238

Hauschildt, J. (1993): Innovationsmanagement, Vahlen, München

Hinterhuber, H./Pechlaner, H. (2001): Mit Erlebniswelten in gesättigten Märkten neue Pionierphasen einleiten, in: Hinterhuber, H./Pechlaner, H./Matzler, K. (Hrsg.): IndustrieErlebnisWelten – Vom Standort zur Destination, Erich Schmidt Verlag, Berlin, p. 11–21

Vivre – Das Nachrichtenmagazin für Genießer (2006): Herr des Kristalls und der Trophäen, Juli/August 2006, p. 70–75

Pechaner, H./Fischer, E. (2006): Alpine Wellness - A recource-based view, in: Tourism Recreation Research, Special issue on "Wellness Tourism", Vol. 31, No. 1, p. 67–77

Pechlaner, H./Fischer, E./Priglinger, P. (2006a): Die Entwicklung von Innovationen in Destinationen – Die Rolle der Tourismusorganisationen, in: Pikkemaat, B./Peters, M./Weiermair, K. (Hrsg.): Innovationen im Tourismus – Wettbewerbsvorteile durch neue Ideen und Angebote, Erich Schmidt Verlag, Berlin, p. 121–137

Pechlaner, H./Fischer, E./ Steiner, O. (2006b): Vom Standort zur Destination – Barrieren und Hindernisse auf dem Weg vom Industrie- zum Dienstleistungsdenken, in: Reuber, P./ Schnell, P. (Hrsg.): Postmoderne Freizeitstile und Freizeiträume – Neue Angebote im Tourismus, Erich Schmidt Verlag, Berlin, p. 77–91

Pechlaner, H., Hammann, E., Fischer, E. (2005a): Leadership und Innovationsprozesse: Von der Kernkompetenz zur Dienstleistung, in Pechlaner, H., Tschurtschenthaler, P., Peters, M., Pikkemaat, B., Fuchs, M. (Hrsg.): Erfolg durch Innovation, Deutscher Universitäts-Verlag, Wiesbaden, p.63–87

Pechlaner, H./Fischer, E./Hammann, E. (2005b): Leadership and Innovation Processes – Developement and Products and Services Based on Core Competencies, in: Journal of Quality Assurance in Hospitality and Tourism, Vol. 6 (3/4), p. 31–59

Prahalad, C. K./Hamel, G. (1990): The core competence of the Corporation, in: Harward Business Review, May/June, p. 79–91

Rogers, E. (1983): Diffusion of innovation, (3rd ed.), Free Press, New York

Tschurtschenthaler, P. (2005): Die gesamtwirtschaftliche Perspektive von touristischen Innovationen, in: Pechlaner, H., Tschurtschenthaler, P., Peters, M., Pikkemaat, B., Fuchs, M. (Hrsg.): Erfolg durch Innovation, Deutscher Universitäts-Verlag, Wiesbaden, p. 3–23

Tourismus in Bayern, Juni 2005, Broschüre des Bayerischen Staatsministeriums für Wirtschaft, Infrastruktur, Verkehr und Technologie

HARALD PECHLANER, CHRISTOPHER REUTER AND ANITA ZEHRER

Innovation Awards in the German Tourism Industry

1   Introduction

Although innovation used to be a rather under-researched field in the tourism industry for a long time (Pikkemaat, 2005), it has become the centre of attention in the last few years. Since the beginning of the new millennium in particular, researchers have increasingly began to discuss innovation in tourism (Hollenstein, 2001; Jacob/Tintore/Auilo/Bravo/Mulet, 2003; Volo, 2004; Flagestad/Hope/Stevensson/Nordin, 2005; Ottenbacher/Gnoth, 2005; Volo, 2005b; Keller, 2006; Novelli/Schmitz/Spencer, 2006; Hall/Williams, 2008). Nowadays, little doubt remains about the importance of innovation for the tourism industry (Tschurtschenthaler, 2005; Pechlaner/Fischer/Priglinger, 2006; Walder, 2006; Keller, 2008) with single tourism businesses as well as destinations competing for new product innovation to gain strategic advantages. Innovative solutions are the key to long-term growth and development (OECD, 2006). One example for the general importance of innovation is provided by Mansury and Love (2008) who found empirical evidence that in the US service sector innovative firms consistently outperform their competitors in terms of growth.

However, tourism still lags behind in creating innovative solutions, which might be due to the low number of licences and patents in tourism as well as problems of free-riding among the big number of tourism stakeholders within a destination (Hjalagar, 2002; Wöhler, 2006). Awards and prizes (these terms will be used interchangeably in this article) however might be a suitable mechanism to generate and empower innovative services and products.

After providing a definition of the term innovation in the context of tourism, specific characteristics of the tourism industry are discussed. Then, authors describe the general development of innovation prizes in Germany and focus on the tourism industry in order to give an up-to-date analysis of the development of tourism innovation awards. Qualitative data for analyzing innovation awards in tourism (part of which can be seen in table 2 in the appendix) was collected through internet desk research and expert interviews with spokespersons for nine major innovation prizes. Both, material from desk research and expert interviews were analysed with content analysis. "Content analysis is a research technique for the objective, systematic, and quantitative description of the manifest content of communication" (Berelson 1952, p. 18). Qualitative content analysis defines itself within this framework as an approach of empirical, methodological controlled analysis of texts within their context of communication, following content analytical rules and step by step models, without rash quantification (Mayring, 2000). Data was analyzed by the authors separately and subsequently controlled for inter-rater reliability. Finally, advantages and disadvantages as well as impacts and importance of innovation awards are discussed. The paper concludes by briefly identifying possible future developments and fields of research.

2   Innovation in Tourism

Innovation seems to be a major driving force for the competitiveness in tourism (Danneels, 2007; Semlinger, 2007; Nordin, 2003). There are a number of definitions of "innovation" in several disciplines, which differ in terms of variety and have different implications. At least in most business contexts, innovation is linked with the growth theory of the economy (Freeman, 1990). While the neoclassical growth theory uses explicit and implicit assumptions to faultless maximisation, the Schumpeterian theory is quite different. According to Schumpeter (1934), innovation depends on the characteristics of the entrepreneur, who is faced with a dynamic economic environment. Basically, Schumpeter (1934) identified five types of innovation: product (1) and process (2) innovations, the utilization of new resource markets (3), new suppliers (4) and the change of market structures (5). These types of innovation can also be found in the service sector as the most important economic driver (see figure 1). Thus, in the field of tourism, product innovation can be achieved on three different levels: at the service level, at attractions' level and at destination level (Pechlaner/Fischer/Hammann, 2005). Likewise process innovation may be accomplished in management, logistics or through network improvement. The usage of new technologies (transportation, internet, etc.) is considered to be an innovation through entering new resource markets; opening new market segments is a suppliers' innovation. Developing new regional markets on the other hand can work both ways: either by utilizing new resource markets or by rendering new sales markets accessible.

Changing market structure (i.e. creating/destroying monopolies) is also regarded to be an innovation.

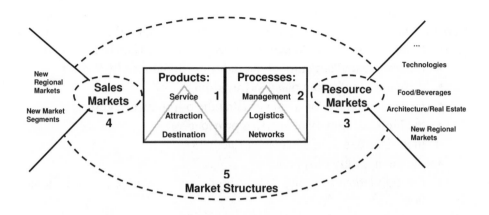

Figure 1: Adaptation of the Schumpeter Model of Innovation to Tourism
(Own elaboration, based on Schumpeter (1934, p. 100f) and Pechlaner/Fischer/Hammann, 2005, p. 35)

The concept of product and process innovation is widely accepted in the tourism industry among various authors (Keller, 2002; Hjalagar, 2002; Volo, 2005a; Pikkemaat/Peters, 2005). But while some remain true to the traditional Schumpeterian typology of the five types of innovation (Peters/Pikkemaat, 2005; Walder, 2006; Hall/Williams, 2008; OECD, 2008), others add marketing (Keller, 2002), management, logistics and institutional innovations (Hjalagar, 1997; 2000), which authors try to apply into the Schumpeterian model (see figure 1).

A distinction is typically made between "invention", "innovation", "diffusion" and "imitation". Hence, while the term "invention" stands for creating something new in general, "innovation" means to successfully establish a new product on the market or to implement a new process into the production cycle of a company. "Diffusion" and "imitation" essentially mean that competitors start to adapt and copy new products and processes (Dosi, 1988; Brockhoff, 1999; Pechlaner/Fischer/Priglinger 2006; Hauschildt/Salomo, 2007). The goal of innovation is a positive change in terms of productivity or added value and to maintain a balance between process and product innovation. However, innovation in the tourism industry differs in many respects from other industries. The travel market is characterized by uncertainties. Due to rapid changes in terms of new technologies, changing consumption patterns of customers and global economic changes, the travel sector has to redefine its business strategies in order to remain competitive. Those and other changes in society have deeply modified the ways in which tourism companies distribute services. The most important reasons for these characteristics however are (Peters/Weiermair, 2002; Pechlaner/Fischer/Hammann, 2005; Pompl/Buer, 2006; Pikkemaat/Holzapfel, 2007; Hall/Williams 2008):

- the fragmented structure of the industry (dominated by SMEs),
- difficulties enforcing patents (free-riding),
- the final product consisting of a bundle of products and services,
- the high complexity of services provided,
- high risks due to high capacity fluctuation,
- the intangibility of services,
- the high labour intensity and the high sensitivity in terms of rising labour costs,
- the low predictability of customers' needs,
- the high degree of customer-integration into the service delivery process, and
- the customer's insecurity about service quality.

These prerequisites lead to two major problems of the tourism industry: (1) first, the low ratio of innovation in tourism which is among the lowest across all branches of the economy; (2) second, the low degree of innovativeness being characterized by small, incremental improvements (Peters/Weiermair, 2002; Pikkemaat, 2005). One way to overcome the difficulties could lie in awards and prizes for tourism innovation. These could balance the market's incompetence to compensate innovators with temporary monopolies (through patents or licenses) in order to coexist with competitors (Hjalagar, 2002; Beritelli/Romer, 2006). All five types of innovation described by Schumpeter could be contact points to initiate innovation awards, though prizes awarded for changing the market structure are highly unlikely.

3 Innovation Awards

The rediscovery of innovation awards: Modern innovation prizes that reward past achievements in different fields of the economy are a rather new development. The *Innovation Award of the German Industry* claims to be the oldest award for industrial products world-wide and even uses this record as a registered trademark (Innovationspreis, 2008). The prize was offered the first time in 1980 and the first winner was the former chemicals company Hoechst

AG which is part of Sanofi-Aventis SA today. A few years later (publicly financed) awards were also established on state level. The first among those was the *Innovation Award of Berlin* in 1984. In the late 1980s and throughout the 1990s other states followed and by 2000 29 awards were offered in Germany and 161 in Europe (STIFT, 2000). Two years later about 60 awards existed in Germany alone, covering all kinds of branches from logistics to the chemicals industry, from textiles to the automotive sector (Bullinger/Schlick, 2002). This type of award is called recognition prize or ex-post-award, as it looks backward, rewarding past achievements (Merrill, 2008).

While the (ex-post) *Innovation Award of the German Industry* claims to be the oldest in the world, the concept behind does have much deeper historic roots. Therefore, we can rather speak about a rediscovery since there have been numerous innovation awards in the past, though with differing purposes and goals. In the Anglo-Saxon literature the first successful innovation prize mentioned is a prize awarded for finding a method to calculate the longitude while navigating the seas (KEI, 2008; Masters/Delbecq, 2008; Merrill, 2008). This prize was offered ex-ante, which means that a certain goal (calculating the longitude) was defined and the first one to solve the problem and accomplish the task (which happened in 1714) was awarded the prize. This type of award is called inducement prize or ex-ante award and looks forward, directing effort at a desired outcome (Merrill, 2008). These prizes differ in terms of how success is measured. Figure 2 gives an overview of the different types of awards.

	Characteristics are **pre-specified (ex-ante)**	Characteristics are **to be discovered (ex-post)**
Success is a **matter of opinion**		**Recognition Prizes**
Success is a **discrete yes/no achievement (first-past-the-pole)**	**Inducement Prizes**	

Figure 2: Typology of General Recognition and Inducement Prizes (Based on Masters/Delbecq, 2008, p. 18 and Merrill, 2008, p. 2)

Although recent studies (e.g. Masters/Delbecq, 2008) show that other forms of prizes (discrete inducement prizes) could possibly be suitable for the tourism industry (e.g. the X-prizes for space travel or the historic example of Charles Lindbergh's first transatlantic crossing in an airplane in 1927, sponsored by the hotel chain owner Raymond Orteig), the article focuses on recognition prizes which have become quite common and are also spread among the German tourism sector.

Innovation awards in the German tourism industry: Although general innovation awards date back to the 1980s, they are a rather new phenomenon in tourism. However, tourism in Germany has seen a rapid development of innovation awards over the last years. The *BTW* (*Bundesverband der Deutschen Tourismuswirtschaft e.V.*) for instance was the first association to offer a tourism prize: the *Innovation Award of the German Tourism Industry* (founded in 2000; the only one founded earlier in 1980 was the *Willy-Scharnow-Prize*, which focused solely on training and education). As far as innovation awards are concerned, a clear distinction is needed to be made between (ex-post) awards mentioned above and (ex-ante) prizes that have a much longer history and (at least in some fields of interest) may have a very promising future (Kalil, 2006). Today, approximately 20 different awards can be identified on national, state and local level (see table 2 in the appendix). Figure 3 gives an overview of the different categories of awards which are relevant to the tourism industry.

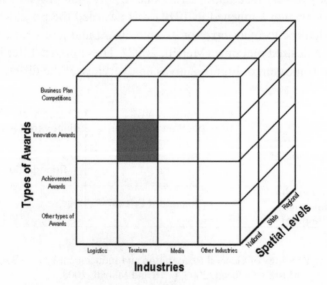

Figure 3: Categories and Types of Recognition Prizes
(Source: Own elaboration)

As far as types and categories of recognition awards are concerned, it must be taken into account that overlaps and interferences might well be possible, e.g. a business plan competition could also include innovative aspects or a logistics company could be awarded a prize by the tourism industry for solving a problem in tourism logistics.

The importance of these single awards cannot be evaluated accurately at this point, since there has been no empirical study on impacts they might have in tourism. Some of the award organizers (e.g. the *German Tourism Association* or the *Association of German Online Travel Portals*) though try to review the impact of their prize, but so far this has either been done without clear methodology or at random. This however does not allow any conclusions to be drawn on a scientific level. On the other hand, it would be too simplistic to merely concentrate on the money awarded to the winners of the different categories (e.g. marketing concepts, product development, etc.), since large monetary prizes are seldom among the existing awards and prizes. The highest ever awarded prize in the German tourism industry is a EUR 50.000 marketing package sponsored by a Munich-based media company for the *Bavarian Innovation Award for Product Development in Tourism*. This prize is only comparable to the general *Innovation Prize of the Bavarian Region of Oberfranken* (Fuchs, 2008). The monetary incentive of other awards is even smaller or non-existent; thus marketing and networking effects seem to be of much higher importance. The participants of the *Sprungbrett* award for instance vote networking as the most beneficial outcome of their participation. Furthermore, the award reduces the risk of the customer to take his or her decision and increases the attractiveness of the potential travel destination or service provider. Hence, the commercial use of the awarded title for marketing purposes is the core-incentive to participate.

Another issue which relates to innovation awards in tourism is multidimensionality. Most awards do not solely focus on innovation, but comprise different aspects of tourism such as marketing, innovation or infrastructural improvements. One way to differentiate the various innovation awards is to use a catalogue on innovation awards developed by the Thuringian Ministry of Economics (STIFT, 2000). Its aim is to check the stability, importance and innovation relatedness of the different awards. The following table lists criteria for assessing and evaluating innovation awards and was adapted to meet the requirements of the tourism sector:

Organisational Features	Selection Process
Founding year	Selection mode
Scope	Selection criteria (number and content)
Number of participants	Importance of innovativeness
Participation requirements	
Amount of prize money	
Frequency	
Jury (number and judges)	

Table 1: List of Criteria for the Assessment of Innovation Awards
(Based on STIFT, 2000, p. 9)

By applying this set of criteria, seven awards could be identified that have a clear focus on innovation (see table 2 in the appendix). However, as can be seen in table 2, the seven identified awards don't follow a stringent pattern, but rather provide very individualistic approaches. While most awards concentrate on a certain aspect of innovative behaviour, others award money to infrastructural projects or focus on product development. The list of possible achievements ranges from scientific research over entrepreneurship to concrete projects. Therefore, innovation awards must be considered from a very broad perspective. Sticking to the criteria defined in table 1 would result in hardly any of the listed awards qualifying as pure innovation awards. For example the *Innovation Award of the German Tourism Industry* is much more of a classical achievement award since it does not put too much emphasis on innovative behaviour, but focuses on industry-wide recognized achievements (in quality or management). Additionally, there is a discussion on the importance of the award's scope (especially for publicly financed Inducement Prizes; NAE, 1999), which implies the issue of whether or not prizes on national level should award international participants and thereby encourage innovative behaviour in other countries. On the other hand, the *German Tourism Award* does not bear the word innovation in its name, but comes close to meeting the proposed criteria, as it highly emphasizes innovation.

During the period of desk research and interviews, authors recognized that some organizers are very restrictive when it comes to providing information about their awards. This however leads to gaps in the identified data and subsequently in the evaluation process, too. Therefore, authors now discuss issues related to the organization and selection process of innovation awards.

Organisation: More than half of the seven identified awards have been founded during the last two years. *TouPLUS*, *Sprungbrett*, the *Bavarian Innovation Award for Product Development in Tourism* (which actually has been re-established after a two year break) and several regional awards are among the most recent awards. Looking at the scope of the awards, national and state prizes are the most common and the most important, while inter-state or even international awards are true exceptions. Bavaria, Brandenburg, Hesse and Thuringia have their own awards while Lower-Saxony has discontinued its prize and Schleswig-Holstein focuses on touristic city projects. Regional prizes are rare in terms of scope and in most cases are rather simplistic in conduct. Nevertheless, their importance for the local tourism environment may not be undervalued.

In tourism, the average number of participants varies widely between a little more than a dozen and close to 100 depending on the award. On the other hand, some well-established innovation awards in technology oriented industries (e.g. the *Innovation Prize of the German Industry*) constantly attract more than 100 participants. However, long-term tendencies or trends cannot be derived from the available data at this point, but it would be of interest to analyze impacts influencing the number of participants. Participation requirements certainly do have an impact on those numbers and vary considerably between the different awards. Some award organizers restrict participation to privately financed projects or focus on start-up companies, while others are completely open to everyone.

This wide spectrum can also be found when it comes to selection criteria: while the *Sprungbrett* Award for internet-based companies even allows projects and business models to compete, others (like the publicly financed *Tourio* in Southern Germany) require that innovation has already been implemented and well established. Hence no generally applicable rules can be deduced from the awards organized in Germany so far. Especially the newcomers like *Sprungbrett*, but also some well-established prizes like the *German Tourism Award* keep working on their set of rules and restructure their awards almost every year.

With regard to fees and prize money one can find the entire range from relatively high fees and no prize money at all (*German Tourism Award*) to the other extreme of no fees at all and high prize sums (*Bavarian Innovation Award*). However, it has already been mentioned that other aspects like networking and marketing opportunities are much greater incentives for participation than monetary incentives are. High fees could even work as high entry barriers rendering the prize (i.e. the brand of the prize) more attractive as not everyone might be able to apply or qualify. In this case, the fees would act as a form of pre-selection before the real competition starts.

In terms of frequency most awards stick to annual and a few to biennial schedules. The selection of the jury however, differs largely. Big juries like the one for the *Sprungbrett* Award (28 jury members) are the exception. Most juries consist of 6–10 members and are a mix of tourism experts, representatives of the sponsors, politicians and public servants (on local or state level).

The selection process: The selection process to determine the winner is the core issue of every competition. Achievement awards are very problematic in this respect as success cannot be assessed in an objective way, but rather is a personal and subjective matter (Masters/Delbecq, 2008). Thus, jury selection and the selection process itself are of utmost importance. While nowadays most awards have no pre-selection, some consider introducing pre-selection criteria to reduce the workload for the jury. In terms of generated publicity it appears to be opportune to have a pre-selection of a certain number of finalists and then to determine the winner in a final event to attract media's attention and promote networking. But as table 2 (see appendix) shows the awards vary in that respect and no standard system has yet been established.

The role of innovation or degree of innovativeness is also extremely diverse. The range goes from innovation being the sole criterion (*German Tourism Award* with nine questions to determine the degree of innovativeness) to awards where innovation only plays an indirect role. First of all it seems important to define and weight the winning criteria. Up to now, the *German Tourism Award* seems to have the most useful approach by defining a set of questions (level of innovativeness or patentability) that assist in rating innovative solutions. This is based on a rather practical definition of innovation in tourism which nevertheless is helpful and exemplary in nature. What is still needed is a method to quantify the influences of those parameters in order to make results more transparent. In general, transparency of the selection process is a critical factor that is still lacking in the case of many awards.

4   Limitations of Innovation Awards in Tourism

Transparency and objectivity are key issues to create functioning and fair competitions with a common participants' approval of award conditions (NAE, 1999). The selection of the jury therefore should be as transparent as possible. The approach of the *Sprungbrett* award, which includes more than two dozen jury members (mostly from the industry), is rather unusual, but it does have two very positive effects. First of all, it enforces networking opportunities between the candidates and the jury members which might help financing the projects. Second, it minimizes political influence which can be problematic in terms of objectivity and might harm the credibility of the competition (NAE, 1999). Another innovative solution of the *Sprungbrett* Award is its electronic voting system which not only allows working with a large group of jury members, but also plays a vital role in minimizing disputes and discussions that could possibly influence the opinion of other jury members.

Besides marketing and networking effects the monetary prize awarded to the winner plays an important role. While most prizes award rather small amounts of money the *German Tourism Award* and the *Bavarian Innovation Award* don't fit into that pattern. While the former builds its entire success and appeal on its well established brand and trademark, the latter awards EUR 50,000 to the award winner. Although research suggests that high prize sums lead to positive signal effects (Davi/Davis, 2004), both strategies work well and attract relatively high numbers of promising candidates.

It is also heavily discussed whether or not award participants belong to the same scope, i.e. that a national contest can or cannot attract international participants (NAE, 1999). In order to create the maximum amount of awareness and to concentrate award efforts, it seems advisable to limit potential participants to the respective award's scope.

In terms of award evaluation, the *Sprungbrett* award is one of the few awards to evaluate its impact by asking jury members and participants about their experiences after the award is finished. However, it would be helpful to conduct longitudinal studies on awards' experiences and improvement opportunities for the benefit of winners and participants. Another issue which is continually discussed is the usefulness of ex-post achievement awards. Some researchers argue that their effect on innovative behaviour is at best incidentally in nature (Merrill, 2008). Economics professor Guy Kirsch once called them rituals and Erwin Staudt, the former head of IBM Germany, even stated that they are "well-meant, but don't have any effect on innovativeness" (cited according to Bullinger/Schlick 2002, p. 363). On the other hand, their advantages in terms of networking possibilities and their marketing effects in terms of trademarks and brand labels can hardly be doubted.

Hence, the question how innovation can be fostered and how prizes can acknowledge breakthrough innovation, especially in challenging services industries like tourism, still needs to be answered. One way to promote innovation could be the integration of inducement prizes into public innovation promotion programs that can work at all scopes from city over regional to state, national and even international level. Figure 4 below gives an overview of such an integrated system to improve a region's innovativeness and competitiveness. The theoretical work done by Keller (2002) and Sell (2000) can be used to identify factors that influence the dynamics of innovation in a region. Inducement prizes could play an active role in further improving the effectiveness of public innovation promotion programs by triggering the foundation of start-up companies and boosting R&D in that region.

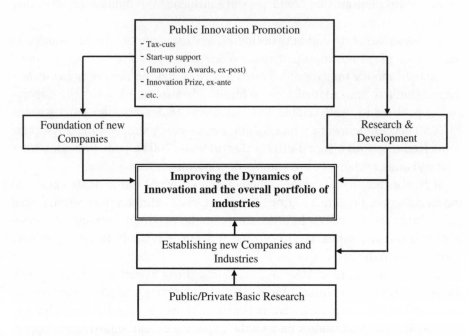

Figure 4: Innovation Prizes as Part of Public Innovation Promotion Programs and General Regional Economic Policy (Based on Keller, 2002, p.190 and Sell, 2000, p. 20)

The basis for such an integrated system is a sophisticated theoretical background, especially regarding the use of inducement prizes to promote innovation in the tourism industry.

5   Outlook

The present paper has certain acknowledged limitations that need to be taken into account when considering the contributions of the study. The most significant limitation is that this is purely a conceptual paper that has discussed innovation awards in tourism. It is apparent that follow-up empirical studies are required to validate and/or modify the issues developed in this exploratory theoretical study. Further research on innovation prizes is necessary to develop a comprehensive understanding of how innovation works in the tourism industry. Especially idiosyncrasies, intangibility or free-riding need to be further researched (Hjalagar, 2002). The next step would be to study whether or not prizes help to overcome obstacles typical for the innovation process in tourism. This however can only be achieved by thorough research on micro- and macroeconomic impacts and effects of prizes. Quantitative data has to be gathered about how the prizes influence winners, destinations and organisers. By then, the following questions might be answered: Do awards spur innovation? How big is the marketing effect generated from winning a well-established prize? What kind of co-operation and networking effects can be found among participants and/or jury members?

If, as some scholars suggest, ex-post recognition awards are in fact useless when it comes to promoting innovative behaviour, the focus in tourism has to be shifted towards inducement prizes. These prizes could be initiated on all levels of scope and for all sorts of innovation as long as their goal is clearly defined. The prizes would need to be well designed (to minimize the higher administration costs) and fulfil the requirements of measurability and credibility (Masters/Delbecq, 2008). So far inducement prizes have only been taken into consideration to develop vaccines, improve agriculture and foster high-tech research (of NASA, DARPA, etc.), but the X-prizes for space travel and various historic samples (KEI, 2008) show that tourism could be an interesting field as well. Davi and Davis (2004, p. 20) even come to the conclusion that "prizes can be used where patent protection for an innovation proves impossible to obtain …". More generally, as with any academic work, it is hoped that the present paper will stimulate other researchers to study the issue of innovation awards in tourism and the role that those can play in securing competitive advantages for tourism service providers. More extensive research is certainly needed in this important area. Authors conclude that the professional use of innovation awards in tourism requires cooperative and synergistic attention with a view to producing memorable product and process innovation.

References

Berelson, B. (1952), Content analysis in communication research. Glencoe.

Beritelli, P./Romer, D. (2006), Inkrementelle versus Radikale Innovationen im Tourismus, in: Pikkemaat, B./Peters, M./Weiermair, K. (eds.), Innovationen im Tourismus, Wettbewerbsvorteile durch neue Ideen und Angebote, Berlin, pp. 53–65.

Brockhoff, K. (1999), Forschung und Entwicklung, München.

Bullinger, H.-J./Schlick, G. H. (2002), Wissenspool Innovation, Kompendium für Zukunftsgestalter, Frankfurt am Main.

Davi, L./Davis, J. (2004), How effective are prizes as incentives to innovation? Evidence from three 20th century contests, Working paper presented at the DRUID summer conference 2004, Retrieved September 8th 2008,
URL: http://www.druid.dk/uploads/tx_picturedb/ds2004-1343.pdf.

Danneels, E. (2007), The process of technological competence leveraging, in: Strategic Management Journal 28, pp. 511–533.

Dosi, G. (1988), The nature of the innovation process, in: Dosi, G./Freeman, C./Nelson, R./Silverberg, G./Soete, L. (eds.), Technical change and economic theory, New York, pp. 221–238.

Drejer, I. (2004), Identifying innovation in surveys of services: a Schumpetrian perspective, in: Research Policy 33(3), pp. 551–562.

Flagestad, A./Hope, C. A./Svensson, B./Nordin, S. (2005), The tourist destination: a local innovation system? The creation of a model, in: Keller, P./Bieger, T. (eds.), Innovation in tourism - creating customer value, St. Gallen, pp. 245–259.

Freeman, C. (1990), The economics of innovation, Hants.

Fuchs, S. H. (2008), Oberfranken, Dokumentation Innovationspreis 2007/08, Bayreuth.

Hall, C. M./Williams, A. M. (2008), Tourism and Innovation, New York.

Hauschildt, J./Salomo, S. (2007), Innovationsmanagement, München.

Hjalagar, A.-M. (1997), Innovation patterns in sustainable tourism, An analytical typology, in: Tourism Management 18(1), pp. 35–41.

Hjalagar, A.-M. (2000), Innovation. In Jafari, J. (ed.), Encyclopedia of Tourism, London, p. 310.

Hjalagar, A.-M. (2002), Repairing innovation defectiveness in tourism, in: Tourism Management 23(5), pp. 465–474.

Hollenstein, H. (2001), Innovation Modes in the Swiss Service Sector, working paper no. 156, Vienna.

Innovationspreis (2008), Innovationspreis, Retrieved November 28th 2008,
URL: www.innovationspreis.com

Jacob, M./Tintore, J./Aguilo, E./Bravo, M./Mulet, J. (2003), Innovation in the tourism sector: results from a pilot study in the Balearic Islands, in: Tourism Economics 9(3), pp. 279–295.

Kalil, T. (2006), Prizes For Technological Innovation, The Brookings Institution, retrieved June 12th 2008,
URL: http://www.brookings.edu/views/papers/200612kalil.pdf.

KEI – Knowledge Ecology International (2008), Selected Innovation Prizes and Reward Programs, retrieved September 8th 2008,
URL: http://www.keionline.org/misc-docs/research_notes/kei_rn_2008_1.pdf.

Keller, P. (2002), Innovation und Tourismus, in: Bieger, T./Laesser, C. (eds.). Jahrbuch 2001/2002. Schweizerische Tourismuswirtschaft, St. Gallen, pp. 179–197.

Keller, P. (2006), Towards an innovation-orientated tourism policy, in: Walder, B./Weiermair, K./Sancho Perez, A. (eds.), Innovation and product development in tourism, Berlin, pp. 55–70.

Keller, P. (2008), Innovation und Tourismus, in: Weiermair, K./Peters, M./Pechlaner, H./Kaiser, M.-O. (eds.). Unternehmertum im Tourismus. Führen mit Erneuerungen, Berlin, pp. 189–204.

Mansury, M. A./Love J. H. (2008), Innovation, Productivity and growth in US business services: A firm-level analysis, in:. Technovation 28, pp. 52–62.

Masters, W./Delbecq, B. (2008), Accelerating prize rewards: History and typology of technology prizes and a new contest design for innovation in African agriculture, Conference paper (Addis Ababa, April 7), retrieved September 5th 2008, URL:http://www.agecon.purdue.edu/staff/masters/MastersDelbecq_AcceleratingInnovation_RevJune2008.pdf

Mayring, P. (2000), Qualitative content analysis, Forum: Qualitative Social Research 2, pp. 1–28.

Merrill, S.A. (2008), Prizes in Science and Engineering: New (Old) Tool for Research and Innovation? Presentation at the 33rd Annual AAAS Forum on Science and Technology Policy (Washington, D.C., May 8), retrieved September 8th 2008, URL: http://www7.nationalacademies.org/step/

NAE – National Academy of Engineering (1999), Concerning Federally Sponsored Inducement Prizes in Engineering and Science, retrieved September 8th 2008, URL: http://www.nap.edu/catalog/9724.html.

Nordin, S. (2003): Tourism clustering and innovation – Paths to economic growth and development, The European Tourism Research Institute, Mid Sweden University.

Novelli, M./Schmitz, B./Spencer, T. (2006), Networks, clusters and innovation in tourism: a UK experience, in: Tourism Management 27(6), pp. 1141–1152.

OECD (2006), Innovation and Growth in Tourism, Paris.

OECD (2008), Tourism in OECD Countries 2008, Trends and Policies, Paris.

Ottenbacher, M./Gnoth, J. (2005), How to develop successful hospitality innovation, Cornell Hotel and Restaurant Administration Quarterly 46(2), pp. 205–222.

Pechlaner, H./Fischer, E./Hammann, E. (2005), Leadership and Innovation Processes – Development of Products and Services Based on Core Competencies. In Peters, M./Pikkemaat. B. (eds.). Innovation in Hospitality and Tourism, Binghamton, pp. 31–58.

Pechlaner, H./Fischer, E./Priglinger, P. (2006), Die Entwicklung von Innovationen in Destinationen – Die Rolle der Tourismusorganisationen, in: Pikkemaat, B./Peters, M./Weiermair, K. (eds.). Innovationen im Tourismus, Wettbewerbsvorteile durch neue Ideen und Angebote, Berlin, pp. 121–136.

Peters, M./Weiermair, K. (2002), Innovationsverhalten im Tourismus, in: Bieger, T./Laesser, C. (eds.). Jahrbuch 2001/2002. Schweizerische Tourismuswirtschaft, St. Gallen, pp. 157–178.

Pikkemaat, B. (2005), Zur empirischen Erforschung von Innovationen im Tourismus, in: Pechlaner, H./Tschurtschenthaler, P./Peters, M./Pikkemaat, B./Fuchs, M. (eds.). Erfolg durch Innovation, Perspektiven für den Tourismus- und Dienstleistungssektor, Wiesbaden, pp. 87–102.

Pikkemaat, B./Holzapfel, E. M. (2007), Innovationsverhalten touristischer Unternehmer: Triebkräfte und Hemmnisse, in: Egger, R./Herdin, T. (eds.). Tourismus:Herausforderung:Zukunft, Berlin, pp. 241–258.

Pikkemaat, B./Peters, M. (2005), Towards the Measurement of Innovation – A Pilot Study in the Small and Medium Sized Hotel Industry, in: Peters, M./Pikkemaat. B. (eds.). Innovation in Hospitality and Tourism, Binghamton, pp. 89–112.

Pompl, W./Buer, C. (2006), Notewendigkeit, Probleme und Besonderheiten von Innovationen bei touristischen Dienstleistungen, in: Pikkemaat, B./Peters, M./Weiermair, K. (eds.). Innovationen im Tourismus. Wettbewerbsvorteile durch neue Ideen und Angebote, Berlin.

95

Schumpeter, J. (1934), Theorie der wirtschaftlichen Entwicklung. Eine Untersuchung über Unternehmergewinn, Kapital, Kredit, Zins und den Konjunkturzyklus, Berlin (1997), 5th reprint of the edition of 1934.

Sell, A. (2000), Innovation und weltwirtschaftliche Dynamik – Der Beitrag der Innovationsforschung nach Schumpeter, Bremen.

Semlinger, K. (2007), Innovationshemmnis „Kundennähe"? – Zur Notwendigkeit einer nachfrageseitigen Ergänzung der keinbetriebsorientierten Innovationsförderung. ZfKE 55(3),
pp. 147–166.

STIFT – Stiftung für Technologie- und Innovationsförderung Thüringen (2000). Innovationspreis Thüringen, Erfurt.

Tschurtschenthaler, P. (2005), Die gesamtwirtschaftliche Perspektive von touristischen Innovationen. In Pechlaner, H./Tschurtschenthaler, P./Peters, M./Pikkemaat, B./Fuchs, M. (eds.). Erfolg durch Innovation. Perspektiven für den Tourismus- und Dienstleistungssektor, Wiesbaden, pp. 3–22.

Volo, S. (2004), Foundation for an innovation indicator for tourism. In Keller, P./Bieger, T. (eds.). The Future of Small and Medium Sized Enterprises in Tourism, St. Gallen, pp. 361–376.

Volo, S. (2005a), A Consumer-Based Measurement of Tourism Innovation. In Peters, M./Pikkemaat, B. (eds.). Innovation in Hospitality and Tourism, Binghamton, pp. 73–88.

Volo, S. (2005b), Tourism Destination Innovativeness. In Keller, P./Bieger, T. (eds.). Innovation in Tourism - Creating Customer Value, St. Gallen, pp. 199–211.

Walder, B. (2006), Sources and determinants of innovation – the role of market forces. In Walder, B./Weiermair, K./Sancho Pérez, A. (eds.). Innovation and Product Development in Tourism. Creating Sustainable Competitive Advantage, Berlin, pp. 7–24.

Wöhler, K. (2006), Wahrnehmung von Innovationen: soziale und kulturelle Aspekte. In Pikkemaat, B./Peters, M./Weiermair, K. (eds.). Innovationen im Tourismus. Wettbewerbsvorteile durch neue Ideen und Angebote, Berlin, pp. 85–95.

Paola Paniccia, Harald Pechlaner and Marco Valeri

The Importance of the Time of Experience in the Innovation of Tourism Business – The Sextantio Albergo Diffuso

1 Introduction

Business innovation depends to a large extent on the learning ability of companies, or rather on their ability of developing both new knowledge and suitable methods of knowledge management. This is especially true in a modern global – and hence complex – context; yet it is not sufficient: the concept of knowledge must also be bound to the concept of time to form an inseparable combination (time-knowledge binomial).

The problem of the "right time" in innovation, seen as the main aim of business development, is mainly a cultural problem, i.e. a matter of time consciousness. The concept of time consciousness goes beyond the mere speed in innovation to ensure variety seeking and favours the timely (rapid) and well-timed (appropriately timed) learning of the ever-changing needs emerging from the context, be they internal or external to the company. Thus, it allows the company to successfully adopt a new behaviour each time the context of reference changes, being absolutely tuned in to the variability of the environment. Time consciousness therefore represents a form of knowledge of the values and expectations expressed both within the company during its development and in its external environment. The significance of such interpretation is evident: time consciousness represents an essential form of knowledge that can be used for guiding the development of a company.

It is however very typical for contemporary organisations to have an unstable knowledge of their reference contexts, so much that their ability of finding their way within these contexts is impaired. It is not sufficient to know to be able to innovate; one must be quick in developing new knowledge and well-timed in its execution. The competitiveness of a tourism busi-

97

ness can be enhanced especially through effective learning, which takes place when a company is allowed to emancipate, develop its autonomy and innovate quickly and at the right time, following a principle of hospitality that considers the social and natural value of its environment without causing disruptions in the general direction of the company's development. If the environment were not taken into consideration, the company would run the risk of starting projects that might become outdated already during implementation, due to an evolved context. Thus, survival of the company itself would be at stake.

The importance of an accurate management of the time-knowledge binomial in the innovation processes of tourism service offers becomes paramount, if another relevant phenomenon is considered attentively: the innovative dynamics of the tourism service offer in a destination seem to be growingly connected to the success of innovation criteria developed in real estate management for increasing the value of a location. The latter is apparently becoming more and more a common objective of both the tourism and the real estate sector. Moreover, this aspect becomes even more important in the current situation, in which fierce international competition leads to the necessity of redefining the way of being and doing tourism business. The recent development of innovative business models in the Italian hotel industry such as the "extended" hotel proves it: here the hotel business plays an increasingly central role, if compared to other accommodation types (including the traditional hotel), and becomes a meeting point between the location and the tourist, mostly coming from abroad.

Sextantio *Albergo Diffuso* is an "extended" hotel, which was founded in 1999 on the basis of an innovative idea by Daniele Kihlgren: refurbish the entire medieval borough of Santo Stefano di Sessanio, located in the mountains of the province of L'Aquila (Abruzzo) at 1250 metres above sea level, within the national park Gran Sasso-Monti della Laga. The innovative character of this idea lies in the fact that Sextantio is not only a hotel, but also a project for promoting the history and culture of an entire location, where service innovation is expertly combined with process innovation, from the point of view of both the real estate and the tourism sector. Sextantio actually represents a tourist destination, even though still in progress. This is mainly due to the lack of appropriate governance in the Abruzzo region and to the ensuing difficulty of starting a cooperation among the different stakeholders in this area. In our specific case, the development of the innovative project Sextantio, which became an example for the entire Italian tourism business, should be fostered, on the grounds of the potential material and immaterial resources brought to the location and also of Kihlgren's proven business skills (especially in the planning and organisation phase).

The geographic and cultural proximity of operators clearly determines the birth of economies that are external to the companies but internal to the systems. Specific resources are thus accumulated and bring localised, nontransferable benefits. These benefits derive from the specific physical capital (natural and historical wealth) and social capital (local culture) of a location (Paniccia, 2006b). Sextantio represents one of the most significant international examples of a company internalising the temporal perspective. Here the social and cultural dimension of time translates into timely and well-timed learning from the internal and external context and determines different aspects: the conception of the innovative idea, the competitiveness of the business (in a time span of barely four years), and the triggering of dynamics of intersystemic coevolution of innovation at the local level. Sextantio has thus realised an extremely valuable innovative project for the local and national tourism system, both from an economic and cultural point of view.

The main aim of the present analysis is to show the importance of the time-knowledge binomial for innovations in the hotel industry from an evolutionary and systemic perspective. Some first reflections on the significance of the relation between location, tourism sector and real estate sector for the creation of value in a tourist destination and, more in general, for the competitiveness of the national tourism system, are laid out. Such relations, even though stressed in Europe, needs careful description and analysis.

2 The Time-Knowledge Binomial as a Source of Innovation in the Tourism Business and its Coevolutionary Potential

The evolutionary conception of the dynamics of business development, starting from the principle of contextualisation (Nelson, Winter, 1982), stresses the need of synchronising the cognitive business dynamics with the variability of the phenomena and characteristics of the internal and external context. This is also a crucial problem for the existence, functioning and innovation (i.e. evolution) (Schumpeter, 1934) of the tourism business (Paniccia, 1999; 2002; 2005; 2006a).

In a historical perspective, which also takes into account its objective character, time is a factor of cultural coevolution of business and environment (in short, called time of experience). It is clear that time is one of the most precious orientating tools of mankind. It combines the objective (mechanistic) and subjective (social and cultural) dimension in a unique, hardly separable unit, which is a product of man's socialisation and rationalisation needs. This holds obviously true also for the tourism business, seen as an organised system of individuals. A company uses time according to its needs – as does the individual – both in relation to itself and to its environment. In tourism this establishes the fundamental concept of social time, i.e. of time as regulating instance and as reference for individuals, groups and complex organisations, as well as of the multiplicity of social times, which is strongly related to the former: each individual and each company inevitably has a perception of the duration of time (and of its quality), which is "lived" and used in different ways.

Time and knowledge are shaped by culture and, by influencing each other, produce rewarding knowledge in terms of innovation and, consequently, of competitive advantage. This bond, which has not yet been analysed in depth in the literature on tourism business, seems indeed worthy of attention. This should be done both in the context of studies analysing the processes for creating and enhancing knowledge in and of tourism enterprises (Senge, 1990; Nonaka, 1991; Argyris, 1975, Paniccia, 2006b) as well as the most recent evolutions in innovation management of tourist destinations (Pechlaner et. al., 2000; 2003, 2005, 2006; Mussner et al., 1999; Rispoli, 2001), where the dynamics of innovation grow stronger thanks to innovative criteria for real estate management that aim at increasing the value of a location (Tronconi et al., 2002; Lovelock, 1992; Muhlebach et al., 1998).

More specifically, in tourism consciousness of time and timeliness allow not only to reduce the time of learning from the local environment to a minimum, but above all ensure the timeliness of learning and the conversion of this accumulated knowledge into innovative large-scale tourism projects. These will be absolutely realistic, because implemented at the right time, i.e. they meet the internal and external expectations and pressures in the company as well as those of the guests. In this way businesses innovate and evolve meaningfully (Tidd et al., 1997; Cafferata, 1995). As already explained, there is a connection binding time to knowledge, in short the time-knowledge binomial, with the aim of creating value in every company (Paniccia, 1999). This bond expresses itself in the – not too late and not to early – learning, which helps steering the evolution of an organisation in a dialectic and synchronic relation with the variability of the environment (co-evolution of business and environment).

The social and cultural dimension of time becomes absolutely crucial in the management of learning in and of tourist organisations as a form of guiding innovation. On the contrary, the physical and mechanistic dimension of time plays a more instrumental role, and gains its specific importance as a form of ordering knowledge within the tourism enterprises, thus strengthening its unity and integrity in case change becomes necessary (Paniccia, 2006a). If innovative responses of a tourism business are to be adequately tuned in to environmental variability, the temporal ordering of learning processes becomes absolutely necessary. This must be conceived and planned by the management in view of a dynamic integration with environmental variability.

The socio-cultural and mechanistic characteristics of time blend and harmonise, because time is not only a sterile mathematic succession of rationally and unambiguously conceived units, it is also a critical succession of experiences, which are based on knowledge. The time of experience is the expression of the dialectic relation between many different cultural values, which a tourism company is confronted with during its evolution. In other words, the time of experience is knowledge which develops in time (hence the time-knowledge binomial). Thus time becomes more than just a simple uninterrupted sequence used only as a unit of measurement; it turns into "experienced" time, the time of interior experience which implies "living" through changes.

From the point of view of tourism innovation management it must be stressed that the dualism between an objective and subjective perspective of time through the harmonious evolution of a tourism company with its environment is mitigated. Indeed, due to the requirements of orderliness, regularity and rapidity of operating processes (decision-making and management processes alike), the need of managing time day by day in an adequately compressed and coordinated way becomes evident. This happens inevitably with the help of mechanistic cultural schemes (time of self-coordination) for the necessary rationalisation of knowledge in the company. Nevertheless, to govern the relation between business and environment, it would be more useful to follow a clearly cultural conception of time, a form of knowledge capable of steering organisational learning in a synchronic and harmonious relation with the variability of expectations and pressures arising in the tourism system. The time of experience therefore is a time dimension that includes both above-mentioned perspectives of observing time, in coherence with the conceptual representation of the dimensions of organisational, generative and adaptive learning (Argyris, Schon, 1978). These two perspectives cannot but coexist – as is also demonstrated by the case under analysis – since the subjective perspective expresses itself in a form of holistic knowledge that also includes the second perspective.

In Italy there are many important opportunities to favour innovation in the tourism service offer. They are an expression of the territory and can be described in short as a synergy between factors of the territorial, natural and institutional context (landscape, favourable climate, cultural traditions and production traditions, especially as regards handicrafts, land use, development of tourist organisations and services, awards and regional trade marks, attentiveness and participation of institutions) and business-specific factors, be they structural (size, number of employees, technological innovations and market innovations, etc.) or related to management and organisational skills, which are reflected by company performance. These factors caused different sectors to converge inside the value systems of several tourist destinations in Italy. The value system of a tourist destination can actually be observed from two points of view: on the one hand, the chain of activities generating value for the guest (Fig. 1), on the other hand, the relation between business actors and institutional actors involved in the process of creating value, where a harmonious and integrated management of time-knowledge in the innovation of tourism companies becomes paramount (Fig. 2).

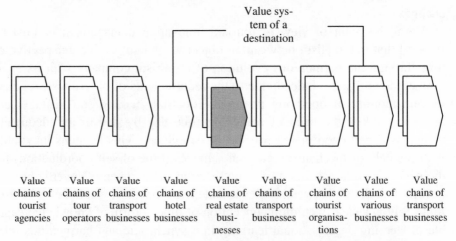

Figure 1: The value chain of a tourist destination (Source: own elaboration)

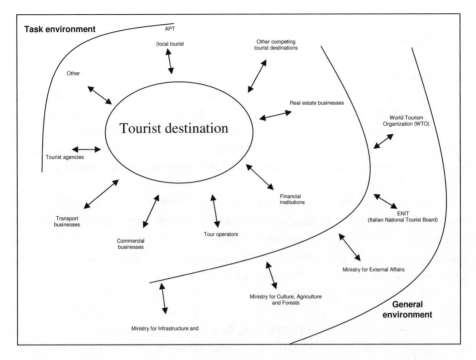

Figure 2: Structure of intersystem relations in the value system of a tourist destination
(Source: own elaboration)

Starting from the chain of all value-generating activities in a tourist destination (Fig. 1) we can draw a preliminary chart – still to be verified by further field studies – of the structure of intersystem relations that characterise tourism product portfolios at the local level (Fig. 2). These relations cover two closely interlinked yet different levels, i.e. a specific and a general level. Each level involves several different business actors and institutional actors and many different relations (of a cooperative or competitive nature), which determine the behaviour of tourism companies in different ways and thus influence the competitiveness of the entire destination.

One of the most notable aspects is the complexity of this structure, which extends beyond the vertical relations within a tourist destination. The specific level concerns all intersystem relations within the local value chain of the tourist destination and, at the same time, extends horizontally over other companies working in competing destinations. This level includes the horizontal relations as well all the intersectoral and intrasectoral relations between the actors in a tourist destination and their socio-economic environment (other companies and local institutions), whereas the general level embraces all relations between the actors of a destination and institutional actors that influence their development.

The purpose of the present paper is to consider the potential of cooperative intersystem relations between the single actors of a destination and between the destination and its socio-economic context of reference, with the aim of reaching that "quality boost in hospitality", which the tourism businesses in the Abruzzo region needed to strengthen their competitiveness on the national and international markets thanks to innovative solutions. At the same time, some important problems in the government of tourist destinations must be solved.

Cooperative relations between tourist (and other) companies and between the former and social institutions can take different forms and are strongly connected to the social and cultural values of their environment. They can be ascribed mainly to the concept of reciprocity that should characterise the process of value generation in every tourist destination.

More in general, in the perspective of enhancing the value of local systems, the relation between business competitiveness and competitiveness of the location in which they operate is to be analysed on the basis of a systemic conception of the territory and of circular relations between different subjects. Next to the structural components (material infrastructure), the development of immaterial components of a location (cultural heritage, technological and managerial skills, services, functions, information, etc.) shall be highlighted, together with the interaction/communication processes between citizens, companies, markets, institutions and local authorities (Saxenian, 1994; Golinelli, 2002). Actions aiming at intensifying relations between tourist companies and companies of other sectors, with the purpose of enhancing the value not only of a tourist destination but also of the entire location, are deemed essential. This is easily understood if we consider that other sectors play a natural role in the completion of developing tourist destinations such as, in particular, the real estate business.

From this perspective the competitiveness of tourism companies and their reference environment would depend to a great extent on the mutual development of the respective relational and coordination skills, in a coevolutionary perspective that aims at generating systemic value (Nahapiet, Ghoshal, 1998; Paniccia, 2002). It emerges clearly that institutions and local authorities can play a key role in the innovation in tourism businesses when fostering integration and cohesion among the different actors of an entire territory.

Among the business actors and institutional actors involved in the value system of a tourist destination, a paramount role is undoubtedly played by the real estate sector with its different actors. The tourism and real estate industries both include various sectors of activity of the local economy and a synergy between the two sectors does indeed exist, but it is not fully fledged yet. They actually interact only on the basis of their mutual functionality. In fact, with a systemic and entrepreneurial approach to tourist destinations, many high-potential synergies between these two sectors can be discovered. The same holds true also of the relation between these two sectors and most other relevant business sectors in a destination (Valeri, 2006). Suffice it to think of the recent development of innovative business methods in the Italian hotel business. In this relation between real estate and tourism the hotel takes on the role of a bridge between the location, the real estate business and the tourist. Such a role becomes even stronger in the most evolved hotel models, in particular the "extended hotel", where product and process innovation in real estate and tourism are skillfully combined. (Tidd et al., 1997).

3   Methodology of Analysis

On the basis of the considerations previously explained, the methodology of the present case study initially focuses on the analysis of Sextantio's dynamics of evolution over a period of about eight years that is from its foundation in 1999 to the present time. This choice represents a viewpoint that still needs to be adequately developed and that differs sharply from other more common and acknowledged ways of observing organisations, which centre, for instance, around the division of labour and specialisation, power relations, communication processes, etc. Nevertheless, it allows to describe the innovative potential in the time-knowledge binomial with respect to generating innovative ideas, establishing a company's short-term competitiveness and also favouring dynamics of intersystemic coevolution for innovation within Sextantio's geographic and social environment.

When analysing Sextantio's dynamics with a view to the time-knowledge binomial, attention was strongly focused on evaluating the synchronic aspects between the dynamics of evolution of the company and the variability of the context as a condition for innovation. To this purpose, the following two aspects were considered together:

- major development projects realised by the company during the period under analysis in response to the evolution of the tourism business in its context of reference;
- ensuing relevant structural changes implemented during the different reference periods of the study, especially as regards timely and well-timed changes in values, principles, working methods and schedules

within the company's operational structure and accommodation facilities.

Attention was focused in particular on the entrepreneur's attitude towards the two factors time and knowledge (forming the concept of time of experience) during the different phases of Sextantio's evolution. The relation between his attitude and the main choices made during the period of reference, mostly going into the direction of a change, was considered. Specific information was gathered on implemented innovations of products and processes in real estate and tourism, with particular reference to their planning and implementation time. The related level of knowledge and competences involved was also taken into consideration.

The study of some historical and sociological material produced around Sextantio was useful, as well as personal communications from the entrepreneur Daniele Kihlgren and the national (Il Sole 24 ORE, Il Messaggero, La Repubblica, Il Tempo) and international specialised press (The American, Financial Times, The Times, The Washington Post), who have written very favourably on Sextantio's strategy. Two further sources of valuable material, documents and information were available, namely the Faculty of Architecture at the University of Pescara and the Museo delle Genti d'Abruzzo (the Museum of the People of Abruzzo) seated in Pescara. The faculty stores several studies and documents on Sextantio's history, in particular its development projects and the structural changes carried out over the years, whereas the museum hosts a rich collection of traditional craft tools, part of which is currently used in Sextantio's arts and crafts workshops. The latter may be considered a proof of cooperation between the company and local institutions, which underlines the cultural and social efforts made by the company to enhance the value of local crafts.

As will be shown later, one of the most interesting aspects emerging from the analysis is Sextantio's cultural attitude, which considers the time factor as an important form of knowledge determining the changes whenever innovation is needed. This growing attitude seems to have recently favoured the planning and implementation of evolution strategies in the perspective of intersystem coevolution on the part of the company: Sextantio itself promoted innovation in a dialectic relationship with its environment. Empirical evidence thus shows how the company was able to understand the material and immaterial factors characterising the multidimensional Abruzzo territory and to enhance their value within its strategic planning, thus turning them into a competitive advantage. All this was not easy in an environment that lacks a culture of entrepreneurship with respect to the new competitive dynamics in tourism.

Based on the interviews carried out, we intend to focus our attention on the value of the time-knowledge binomial in the innovation of the hotel business from an evolutionary and systemic point of view. Special attention shall be paid whenever needed for an adequate governing of relations between hotel businesses, real estate businesses and location with a view to increasing the value of a tourist destination.

4 Sextantio's Innovative Idea: From Evolution to Intersystem Coevolution

Sextantio s.r.l.[5] was founded in 1999 by Daniele Elow Kihlgren, an Italian-Swedish entrepreneur, with the intention of creating an "extended" hotel within the long-deserted ancient borough of Santo Stefano di Sessanio in the Abruzzo region. The accommodation structure is scattered over an area of 3,500 square metres, that is 35 % of the total surface of the borough.

For the national and international tourism service offer system Sextantio represents a new way of being and doing tourism business: it markets an innovative hospitality model that is strongly rooted in its territory and culture. These in turn become basic components of the services offered to the tourist, seeing that the rooms are situated in ancient refurbished buildings. The entire complex consists of 46 rooms, native arts and crafts workshops, a wine cellar selling local products and wines, a restaurant serving typical dishes of the Abruzzo mountains, a wellness centre, an excursion centre and a conference room.

The basic idea of Sextantio already implied the consciousness of the social and cultural dimension of time, seen as a form of knowledge of tourism demand in the national tourism system: these required new accommodation models, such as the "extended" hotel. Furthermore, after the company's foundation that expertly joined timely and well-timed action, the entrepreneur followed a business style which was new to that time and territory and rose from a holistic cultural concepts including on the one hand attentiveness for the social aspects and on the other hand business efficiency. The idea seems indeed to have sprung from a dialectic relation within the context of reference. It was then rapidly transformed into a realistic plan that anticipated possible competitors in the location and was realised at the right time with regard to the needs of (mostly foreign) tourists. All this turned into an inno-

---

5   Initialism for *società a responsabilità limitata*, limited company.

vative offer within the hotel business, because Sextantio's accommodation units are scattered over a large area, but even more so because it increases the value of the landscape as well as the human, historical and artistic resources and attractions of the location.

If we follow the company's evolution over time, we can say that the first important result of Daniele Kihlgren's efforts in terms of time and knowledge was purchasing and refurbishing the buildings in the borough with the intention of preserving as much as possible of the original features, as a necessary condition for ensuring high-quality future hospitality, once they were turned into hotel rooms. The desire of preserving the original function of historic buildings went so far as to maintain clear traces of the past in the plaster and layers of the buildings.

Kihlgren expertly and timely found the necessary financial resources by selling family property and land and prepared to face a series of legal and financial problems in an area historically almost exclusively dedicated to farming. Later, a big project was started in collaboration with important local institutions (such as the Faculty of Architecture at the University of Pescara, the Museo delle Genti d'Abruzzo, the authorities of the national park Gran Sasso e Monti della Laga, the Abruzzo region, the province of Pescara and the municipality) and real estate companies with the aim of preserving the original buildings of the borough. Also, it was to be avoided that the borough's new destination of tourism enterprises cause a mixing of styles in the refurbished buildings or that non-mediaeval furniture, different in type and style, be used in the rooms.

The restoration of all authentic details in the original buildings implied eliminating later architectonic elements, substituting the missing ones with similar elements found in the same region and restoring very delicate parts with the help of the most advanced technologies. Still, these massive interventions remain mostly invisible to the eye. The effort described here was the first evident signal of the business having a temporal perspective that looks to the future as well as a strong sense of timing. Indeed, thanks to these two characteristics the company grew rapidly and steadily and became a real attraction, mostly for foreign tourists.

From the point of view of an adequate management of time and knowledge for the creation of value in a tourist destination, the entrepreneur showed his ability to anticipate future events and their consequences from the very first phase of activity. This allowed him to timely develop all available knowledge and use it at the right time in order to evaluate the future development of his company in relation to the future scenarios in the tourism business (coevolution of business and environment).

Nowadays the tourism business is more and more oriented towards satisfying an expert and demanding public, whose attraction is not captured exclusively by ancient monuments but also by folklore and the anthropological or cultural aspects of tradition. Sextantio's guests can indeed plunge into the local culture of Abruzzo by taking part in the life of the borough and thus discover feelings and emotions that are triggered by its fascinating and unspoiled nature. Today, tourists at Sextantio can stay in houses and buildings that were refurbished with the idea of making them become real homes and where many aspects, such as walls, rooms, doors and windows, furniture and installations differ from those usually found in traditional accommodation structures.

The results described above are no doubt a consequence of a dialectic process – of a mainly cultural nature – between the company and its environment. This was one of Sextantio's characteristics from its very beginning, which progressively grew and developed in time. Furthermore, it all happened against the background of a rather limited degree of complexity of the Abruzzo tourism sector and of the related time model (i.e. the way of understanding and managing time in tourism).

The speed and timeliness with which – even radical – changes where successfully implemented over time on the hotel's operational structure so as to meet the new conception of the "extended" hotel and, even more, the increasingly rapid development of the company itself, with an ever-growing presence of international tourists, are clear signals of an extraordinary ability of double synchronisation (cultural and mechanistic) with the environment. On the one hand the company's management proved its ability to tune in to its internal and external time schedule. This allowed Sextantio to plan the right (timely and well-timed) changes in the original business structure. On the other hand the company showed an extraordinary ability of scheduling time within its operational structure and thus made the implementation of the plans made by the management actually possible.

All this proves that the business acted at the right moment, enhancing its circular dialectic relation with the environment with a view to attaining inter-system coevolution. A fundamental role was played by Kihlgrens business style and culture that would turn Sextantio into an important reference example in the national and international history of tourism and identify a new role of the hotel business and the entrepreneur in the economic, social and cultural local context. Kihlgrens expert capacity of planning with an eye toward future developments actually turned Sextantio into a model of territorial management, which aims at the social and economic revitalisation of the local territory, also through the creation of a new local entrepreneurship. In the near future more traditional arts and crafts workshops will be opened (gold-smithing, weaving, pillow lace production and ceramics) and use authentic antique tools, loaned for free to the senior citizens in the borough. Adjacent lands will be purchased to grow typical local crops and produce local special-ity food (lentils, chickpeas, spelt, pecorino cheese, black truffles and high-quality pasta). Varieties that were given up or disappeared in other locations but not in this historically isolated area (such as e.g. almonds or the crocus sativus used to produce saffron) are also cultivated.

This should suffice to show as to how Sextantio introduces an innovative tendency, if compared to other traditional hotel businesses in this area that are rather isolated from their context of reference, by trying to establish a connection with its environment and by taking into account ethical, social, cultural problems even beyond the strict interests of the business and market. The company thus managed to evolve over the years and innovate in a highly complex environment without losing its autonomy and identity. Furthermore, it managed to adhere more and more to a perspective of intersystem coevolu-tion and to foster useful innovation for the economic and cultural progress of the local and national society. Even though the newly created local conditions attracted tourism and therefore fostered a longer stay of the tourists in the whole region, the empirical analysis shows that this destination still needs to fully express its potential.

Summing up the elements of the analysis laid out in the preceding para-graphs, the distinctive competences lying beneath Sextantio's success can be described as follows:

- expert timely and well-timed planning abilities within a model of terri-torial management that aims at revitalising society and economy in the Abruzzo region, also by promoting the rise of a new local entrepre-neurship;
- extreme attentiveness to relationships with the local real estate compa-nies for the restoration of the original buildings in the borough;
- philological approach to some aspects of the indigenous material cul-ture that survived in the memory of the senior citizens (wool mat-tresses, bed linen and tablecloths woven on traditional looms, blankets dyed with natural colours);
- use of complex modern but unobtrusive technologies (remote con-trolled low-voltage electrical installations, remote controlled radiant floor heating, intranet, internet, satellite TV).

All these competences show the company's extraordinary attitude for sys-temic innovation. This raises some first considerations on the delicate relations existing between tourism companies, real estate companies and their location when planning to enhance the value of a tourist destination, which are set out in the subsequent section.

5 The Relation between Tourism Business, Real Estate Business and Their Location when Planning to Enhance the Value of a Tourist Destination

If we analyse a tourism destination from a systemic and entrepreneurial perspective, the "extended" hotel becomes a meeting point between the location, the real estate business and the tourist. This is part of the reason why Sextantio managed to expertly join product innovation and process innovation, both from the point of view of the real estate business and the tourism business. The organisational model of the "extended" hotel actually stresses the importance of the bond existing between the dynamics of tourism and of the real estate business. On the one hand, the accommodation sector is attracting more and more investments from real estate companies and operators, on the other hand, the hotel businesses are not only looking for investments from the real estate sector but first and foremost for real estate entrepreneurship. This would allow to increase the value of entire locations by means of a human and structural resource development that aims at boosting real estate revenues as a means of enhancing the value of the hospitality offered.

The case study described in this paper clearly shows the influence of the Abruzzo territory on Sextantio's competitiveness in attracting foreign tourists. Such influence seems to be grounded in the hotel's high-quality hospitality as well as the natural, historic and artistic sights of the region, rather than being an achievement of the current local government. In fact, up until now the latter has shown very limited management competences. Suffice it to consider the scarce activity of local marketing: Sextantio would have been able to manage its relation with the market in a much better way, had the conditions been different. This is partly the responsibility of Sextantio, but mostly of the local and national institutions that proved to be rather indifferent to the company's innovations and their possible positive effects on the value of the local (but also national) tourism business. Even worse, they sometimes even inhibited them.

As long stated in the relevant literature, regional marketing is characterised by a potentially very close-knit network of relations and information and may therefore represent a first important step toward enhancing the value of a tourism company (in particular, of Sextantio) and its location. This may be a necessary condition, but it certainly is not sufficient. It should not be forgotten that a company's visibility is related mainly to its ability of rationalising activities and production processes. This is not only expressed by the use of advanced (standardised) technologies, but goes beyond the boundaries of the single company and therefore requires entrepreneurs to have a good relational attitude and sense of coordination with their environment.

Adequate cooperation strategies among involved operators should indeed be developed and should first and foremost foster the growth of the Italian tourism business as regards both the technical and cultural aspects. This seems to represent a key factor in consolidating the success of a tourist destination and its dynamics of innovation. In short, two aspects must be taken into account at the same time: how to enhance the economic value of territorial factors and how to manage and organise small tourism companies in a way that allows them to compete in an enlarged market. This would have positive effects on the preservation and valorisation of the historic, social and cultural resources of countries sporting many traditional products (like many European countries), some of which reach peaks of excellence, especially in Italy.

Against the background of these new complex scenarios and our analysis, some basic aspects of the proposed case study seem worthy of further in-depth studies with a view to the innovation processes in the tourism business. A study of the structure, management and organisation of tourist businesses, as well as the actual and potential role of entrepreneurs should be carried out within each tourism business sector, with a strong focus on management. The study should centre on the processes of knowledge creation and management that are aimed at enhancing the competences of leading companies in a destination and of companies that are not tied to any particular destination. In addition, attention should be focused on the real and potential network of inter-system relations (structure and typology of relations) existing between different tourism companies and other businesses in a specific local environment. It is important to enquire whether the differences in the competitive dynamics of various tourist destinations within the same nation can indeed be ascribed to the different elements, especially immaterial elements, in the local environment of each tourist destination. Finally, the role and characteristics of local government institutions in creating and developing adequate relations within specific tourist destinations should be examined on a larger scale. Their role in promoting coevolutionary dynamics between the local tourism companies and other businesses and between the former and the economic and social environment should be investigated. At the same time, the institutional and market-related aspects on which to base innovation could be identified for each specific tourist destination, so that systemic value be generated in the perspective of global competition in the tourism sector.

6   Conclusions

The evolutionary dynamics of Sextantio doubtlessly represents a proof of how the interaction between the dynamics of time and knowledge may contribute to creating business value trough innovation, if adequately managed in a systemic perspective. The present analysis describes the sometimes very deep influence of the time-knowledge binomial on the harmonious evolution of a company with its environment. The time of experience is shown to play an essential role in structuring the actual strategic and operational behaviour of a company. Sextantio's history itself indicates that it is the awareness of the social and cultural dimension of time and of the more instrumental role played by the mechanistic dimension that fosters the above-mentioned relation between a company and its environment. The company is thus able to timely plan innovative projects that follow the evolution of the tourism system and, more important, to implemently them at the right time without disrupting its unity and integrity.

These premises undoubtedly boosted the development of the circular dialectic process between the company and its environment. Sextantio consequently managed to progressively enter a conscious relation of intersystem coevolution with its environment and to assert its innovative tradition as well as its importance for the economic and cultural progress of the national and local tourist system. Sextantio's experience shows that the possibility of creating value through innovation depends on an appropriate systemic governance of the territory, beside the company's structural capability of meeting the needs of its environment autonomously, following an adequate strategy and time schedule and – before that – the ability of triggering a process of intersystem coevolution with the location on the basis of an integrated vision of time and knowledge.

The lack of adequate governance lies at the origin of many disruptions between the innovative tourist products and competitiveness. As supported also by the results of the present study, we think two main factors are to be held responsible for this:

The first factor is entrepreneurship in the Italian tourism business, which will grow progressively as various tourist destinations in different locations manage to close the gap between their traditional strong points and a renewed planning ability of their entrepreneurs, who must take into account the most recent competitive dynamics in the tourism business.

The second factor can be ascribed to the supporting role of institutions and their ability of adapting and growing to create the preconditions for a qualitative development of small tourism companies over time and thus enhance competitiveness of the Italian tourism sector as a whole. One of these conditions seems to be paramount, i.e. the role played by the "meta-organisers" for the competitive development of small tourism companies in particular. In other words, the role played by local institutions, which should create and support long-term relations with the companies operating in a specific context and at the same time foster relations among the single companies (Rullani, 1999).

If the conditions are right, the rediscovery and valorisation of innovative tourist products in a modern tourism system, which typically has a high degree of complexity and industrialisation as well as a progressive standardisation of services, represents an opportunity of renewing competitiveness in the entire national system by stressing specific and authentic local traditions. Such products are indeed an expression of the historical and cultural values of a country and of a tourist destination with the real estate sector playing a central role.

References

Argyris C. (1975), Il leading-learning: cos'è e come svilupparlo, in: Problemi di gestione, vol. XX, n. 3.

Argyris C., Schon D.A. (1978), Organizational Learning: a Theory of Action Perspective, Addison Wesley, Reading Mass

Cafferata R. (1995), Sistemi ambiente e innovazione. Come si integrano la continuità e il mutamento nell'impresa, Giappichelli, Torino.

Golinelli M.C. (2002), Il territorio sistema vitale, Giappichelli, Torino.

Lovelock C.H. (1992), Managing Services: Marketing and Human Resource, London.

Muhlebach R.F., Alexander A.A. (1998) Business Strategies for Real Estate Management Companies, Chicago.

Mussner R., Pechlaner H., Schönhuber A. (1999), (eds.), Management della destinazione, Rüegger, Chur-Zurich.

Nahapiet J., Ghoshal S. (1998), Social Capital, Intellectual Capital and the Organizational Advantage, in: Academy of management Review, vol. 23.

Nelson R.R., Winter S.G. (1982), An Evolutionary Theory of Economic Change, Harvard University Press, Cambridge, Mass.

Nonaka I. (1991) The Knowledge-creating Company, Harvard Business Review, November-December.

Paniccia P. (1999), Il tempo nel governo dell'impresa industriale. Tempo e conoscenza nell'economia delle imprese, Giappichelli, Torino.

Paniccia P. (2002), Dinamiche temporali e cognitive nell'approccio sistemico al governo dell'impresa, Cedam, Padova.

Paniccia P. (2005), Organizzazione che apprende, crea e valorizza la conoscenza, in: Cafferata R. (ed.) Organizzazione e direzione aziendale, Aracne, Roma.

Paniccia P. (ed.) (2006/a), Creazione e valorizzazione della conoscenza, Aracne, Roma.

Paniccia P. (2006/b), Istituzioni e mercato nella gestione e nella competitività delle imprese rurali del Lazio: le imprese coricole della provincia di Viterbo, in: Ciappei C., (ed.) La valorizzazione economica delle tipicità locali tra localismo e globalizzazione, Firenze University Press, Firenze.

Pechlaner H., Weiermair K. (eds) (2000), Destination management. Fondamenti di marketing e gestione delle destinazioni turistiche, Touring Editore, Milano.

Pechlaner H., Weiermair K., Laesser C. (eds) (2003), Politica del turismo e destination management, Touring University Press, Milano.

Pechlaner H., Fischer E., Hammann E. (2005), Leadership and Innovation Processes – Developement and Products and Services Based on Core Competencies, in: Journal of Quality Assurance in Hospitality and Tourism, vol. 6 (3/4).

Pechlaner H., Fischer E., Priglinger P. (2006), Die Entwicklung von Innovationen in Destinationen – Die Rolle der Tourismusorganisationen, in: Pikkemaat B., Peters M., Weiermair K. (eds): Innovationen im Tourismus – Wettbewerbsvorteile durch neue Ideen und Angebote, Erich Schmidt Verlag, Berlin.

Rispoli M. (ed.) (2001), Prodotti turistici evoluti. Casi ed esperienze, in: Italia, Giappichelli, Torino.

Rullani E. (1999), I contesti che facilitano le relazioni: i meta-organizzatori fra imprese ed istituzioni, Convegno Sinergie, Università degli Studi della Calabria, 9th-10th September.

Saxenian A. (1994), Regional Advantage, Harvard University Press.

Schumpeter J.A. (1934), The Theory of Economic Development, Harvard University Press, Cambridge.

Senge P. (1990), The fifth Discipline. The Art and Practice of the Learning Organization, Doubleday Dell Publishing Group.

Tidd J., Bessant J., Pavitt K. (1997), Managing Innovation. Integrating Technological, Market and organizational Change, John Wiley & Sons Ltd., Chichester.

Tronconi O., Ciaramella A., Pisani B. (eds) (2002), La Gestione di edifici e di patrimoni immobiliari. Asset, property e facility management. Analisi, modelli operativi ed esperienze a confronto, Il Sole 24 ore.

Valeri M. (2006), Un approccio di filiera sistemico-imprenditoriale per l'analisi della competitività delle imprese rurali, in: Ciappei C., (ed.) La valorizzazione economica delle tipicità locali tra localismo e globalizzazione, Firenze University Press, Firenze.

FRANK M. GO AND RONALD ISRAELS

Innovation of Care and Cure in the Netherlands

1   Introduction

Evidently, healthcare has become an urgent, recurring and dominant political issue. The U.S. media portrayal of the healthcare situation played, for instance, a critical role in the U.S. presidential elections of 2008. "Obama, McCain trade jabs over taxes and healthcare", stated a headline of the Wall Street Journal just days after the candidates had their final debate at Hofstra University in Hempstead New York (Wall Street Journal, 2008).

In this chapter we propose that healthcare issues are not limited to the U.S, but rather have a universal character. For example, in the Netherlands the functioning of the healthcare system has become increasingly negatively portrayed in the media. There is a general sense of urgency for healthcare provision that is better, faster and affordable. These signals about disruptive change from the fringes of the current market afford the travel trade, a sector with practice and performance that differs substantially from the healthcare sector, to create new demand. An obstacle to raise the level of innovation is the perceived risk within traditional organizations, particularly in the healthcare sector. The role of innovation in the healthcare sector is "getting a better edge to dealing with problems of" illness (Tidd et al, 2001:19). By picking up signals and translating these to innovations healthcare providers can develop variations on an established theme and may find relevance in the newly emerging opportunities. For instance, healthcare travel, whilst still emerging and therefore difficult to interpret for some presents a potential trigger for innovation. The challenge is to identify a means to resolve the innovator's dilemma (Christensen (1997) to build the structures and align the processes which enable organizations to ride the horse of "continuity" and "change". Accordingly, the main argument developed in this chapter is that healthcare providers should learn to master the "steady state" doing what we already do better (Tidd et al, 2001) and absorb "new" knowledge from the travel trade to make health travel work in practice. This chapter seeks to raise awareness amongst policymakers and decision makers involved in the healthcare provision and their suppliers of goods, ideas and services, for the urgent need to raise the level of innovation in the healthcare chain. In particular this chapter will:

- Examine how "crisis" in the healthcare sector triggers an urgent need for innovation
- Describe, using the case of Dutch healthcare practice, how the perspectives of the healthcare market are changing and create opportunities for the healthcare sector and the travel trade to pick up signals and translate them to healthcare travel innovations
- Illustrate through novel Cure and Care concepts how the market is changing
- Identify for levers to enable the implementation of those new healthcare concepts that are necessary to achieve optimal healthcare travel solutions.

2   Need for Innovation

All stakeholders in het global healthcare system have to find effective solutions to provide better quality to more people at lower cost. "In some ways, the healthcare ecosystem is a victim of its own success. Innovations in disease diagnosis, treatment and early intervention have helped lengthen life spans, fend off dire threats and produce an overall expectation of steady progress to the eradication of disease. Due to its very nature, there is also a societal expectation that healthcare be universally accessible" (IBM, 2004). In more simple words: the current organization of healthcare is unsustainable (Shimo, 2006).

The following illustrations endorse the question whether contemporary healthcare can be sustained in its present format:

- In the US Healthcare expenditure is expected to rise form 15 % (2004) to 18 % (2010) (IBM, 2004).
- In US the Hospital Image is:
- "Staff is on strike, laid-off, or Angels of Mercy
- Large, cold, unresponsive institutions
- Work is stressful, highly structured, and un-fun
- Tied to a professional career, not open to change" (O'Neil)
- In 2006 where nearly 3 percent of Canada's population on waiting lists for medical treatment, and experts predict the list will grow as the population ages. In 2004, the Conference Board of Canada reported that

healthcare already consumes close to a third of all provincial revenues, and by 2020 this figure is projected to climb to 44 percent, just to maintain current levels of service (Shimo, 2006, p. 34).

- The Netherlands is the only country with a healthcare system that is privately financed, but, oddly, has rather long waiting lists and high costs at the same time. A recently issued report for the healthcare improvement platform "Better Faster" (Sneller Beter) notes, that the latter is strange, because, in general, privately financed systems are characterized not only by high cost, but also short waiting lists (Scheepbouwer, 2006). The same report goes on to state, that without any efficiency improvements one in five people in the Netherlands by 2025 would have to work in healthcare while healthcare productivity would continue to decline in comparison with other countries. The report predicts healthcare curative costs will rise up to EUR 57 billion a year in 2020 from the present EUR 21 billion (5.3 % of GDP). Savings can be realized by process improvement (examples: better treatment plans, better procurement, and saving on overhead costs). The potential for improvement is calculated to EUR 20 billion a year by 2020. But cost will still be EUR 37 billion a year, EUR 16 billion more then the present costs.
- In the report "Verklaringsmodel verpleging en verzorging 2007" (SCP, 2007) is calculated that between 2006 and 2030 the demand for caring in the Netherlands will rise with 34 %. In de same period the growth of the amount of people over 65 will rise 63 %.

The global healthcare system faces a formidable challenge namely a transformational and fundamental change of the system to provide care and cure. Whilst numerous examples of solutions can be cited, some of the more credible ones are seen to be:

- Refocusing healthcare forms of acute care to chronic care to preventive and predictive care (IBM, 2004). The basic thought of this shift is: If you can predict illness, you can prevent it.
- Combining medical expertise with entrepreneurship so as to enable responsiveness to open markets, freedom of choice in type of treatments, and electronic patient dossiers represent positive drivers for the development of a more transparent healthcare system that functions better and faster. Because a customer centric approach enables consumers to make informed choices and allows care providers to boost their performance (Scheepbouwer, 2006).

- As a result of globalization a lot of innovation solutions arise for healthcare provisioning. The latter represents a long road (Ueng, 2006) but in The Netherlands potential patients are not negative about health-care provided outside The Netherlands (Nivel, 2004). In general (non specific healthcare related) there are concerns in The Netherlands about global reallocation of work but reported is that the benefits are more important then the risks and additional policies to prevent this will not work (CPB,2005).

In summary, spiraling costs are transforming the structure of Dutch health-care providers into a dynamic and challenging arena with plenty of opportunities and in great need for innovative solutions. The challenge in the arena for healthcare provision may be summarized by three priorities. These are:
1. The need to decrease cost and manpower:
   - Lower costs in general and specific in case of not insured treatments
   - Lower insurance costs, where the consumer accepts restriction to the choice of treatment methods and locations
2. The need to ensure the quality of customer treatment:
   - The customer expects always excellence and low risks when using healthcare.
   - In search of excellence the customer is willing to search and travel for global solutions
   - The quality of service (the caring) becomes at least as important as the quality of curing
3. The need to decrease throughput cycle time
   - The customer does not want to wait before any treatment and wants fast recovery afterwards.

3   Changing Perspectives

The central question in this section is: How is the centre of gravity changing, in general terms, within the Dutch healthcare market? Exhibit 1 offers a framework which contrasts the various factors in the traditional dominant perspective column against an emerging, new perspective on the Dutch healthcare market. The former represents the value-adding idea in the minds of all healthcare stakeholders, i.e., until recently. Presently, the new perspective supports a decentralized market approach which, in turn, enables consumers to participate in making decisions that matter to them.

	Traditional dominant perspective	New perspective
1	Public	Market
2	Group	Individual
3	Real	Virtual
4	Local	Global
5	Cure	Care
6	Acute treatment	Perfective, Preventive
7	Certain / Assured	Uncertain / Unassured
8	Closed (expert knowledge)	Transparency (consumer knowledge)

Figure 1: Traditional dominant perspective vs. new perspective

Explanation by perspective
1. *Public vs. market* – The healthcare in The Netherlands used to be a completely government regulated market, wherein insurance, prices and policies were defined by the government. The withdrawal of government has caused more private entrepreneurial involvement in the healthcare market.
2. *Group vs. individual* – The Dutch healthcare market was characterized by a group-oriented market approach, wherein the choice of care followed the habit of the group (religion, political choice). The latter has changed in favor of the individual choice for a particular physician. It is expected that this trend toward greater individualization will continue n future. At one extreme end of the group-individual continuum the consumer may be portrayed as an expert capable of diagnosing his own disease and opt for the best possible remedy.
3. *Real vs Virtual* – Until recently consumers had to visit their physician and/or hospital to receive their treatment. Today, the development of information and communication technologies affords consumers to communicate with one or more physicians across the world without travelling. Also operations and parts of the caring will be possible without the real presence of the treating physician or in some case without leaving your home.
4. *Local vs. Global* – Traditionally, healthcare was provided in the neighborhood. Often in walking distance of the consumer's residence. But the latter has changed. At present the Dutch healthcare system is becoming increasingly centralized, in part, as a result of the scaling of regional - and university hospitals. For special (rare) diseases Dutch healthcare is de facto already nationalized. Beyond that a "global" scenario is emerging, due to long waiting lists and new types of treatments that are offered abroad.

Increasingly, Dutch patients travel to Belgium and Germany or to Spain and Turkey which offer care quality travel at relatively low costs.

5. *Cures vs. Care* – Nowadays healthcare may be seen as cure-oriented. The physician, medicines and curing technologies are now the central focus in the healthcare system, wherein the *care* serves as a support component. After-care takes place for the most part in hospitals which by contemporary consumption standards are seen to be both expensive and of relative poor quality. For this reason caring centers in the Netherlands are developed in combination with existing hospitality facilities (including hotels and leisure chains). Such development enhances not only the quality of the care but also helps to lower the total cost of the curing and caring process. Healthcare travel may be seen as an exponent of the latter development.

6. *Acute vs. Perfective and Preventive treatment* – Western healthcare is oriented toward acute treatment. To avoid increasing cost of healthcare orientation to more preventive certain measures are needed. In contrast to the increased use of perfective treatments such as plastic surgery, which tend to contribute to a cost increase of healthcare. Because the majority of insurance companies does not compensate for perfective treatments, they tend to follow an individualized path, wherein the urge of efficiency is very important and highly likely to accelerate the aforementioned changes.

7. *Certain / Assured vs. Uncertain / Unassured.* For an individual in The Netherlands healthcare was almost unlimited assured and the quality seemed to be of unlimited quality. Individuals where not aware of incidental and structural failures of the healthcare system. By the above mentioned changes the outcome of healthcare will be less certain and not always assured by an insurance company. Consumers will need new methods to ascertain and assure their self.

8. *Closed (expert knowledge) vs. Transparency (consumer knowledge)* – Healthcare was in The Netherlands a closed system where the professionals (physicians) decided the diagnosis and which treatment was necessary on which moment on which place. By increased complexity of healthcare (demand and supply) and increased access to information (all over the world) the client will know the best which treatment is necessary on which moment on which place advised by the physicians in which he has trust.

The above changing perspectives, particularly the shift in the centre of gravity from local – to global healthcare services afford health care providers to connect with the travel trade to resource the knowledge transfer option by exploiting it. Furthermore, the change from a government regulated health-care system towards a market orientation implies more private entrepreneu-rial involvement and competition for healthcare providers. The age of global networks present same with a sense of urgency for a rethink of "old" re-sponses in a rapidly changing environment. Particularly, the shift in power away from hierarchical organizations towards networks of customers and suppliers for joint value creation affords the current stakeholders (govern-ment, insurance companies, hospitals, physicians) and new stakeholders such as the travel trade - and facility-providers ample opportunity for innovation. Some examples of potential innovation are described in the next section.

4   Novel Cure and Care Concepts

In this section healthcare travel solutions are described which are relatively new concepts for the Dutch Healthcare market. These concepts are developed to act on the need for changes described in section 2. Moreover, they can be seen also as an illustration of the changed perspectives as chronicled in sec-tion 3. The feasibility of the concepts corroborates the changed perspectives.

   To understand these solutions at first 'healthcare travel' as general con-cept to innovate healthcare is explained.

4.1   Healthcare Travel

Healthcare travel is (in the Wikipedia called Medical tourism but also re-ferred to as "healthcare tourism") is a term which describes the rapidly-growing practice by consumers of travel across international borders for the healthcare purposes (Wikipedia, 2008). Healthcare travel can be seen as "a deliberate attempt on the part of the tourist facility or destination to attract tourists by promoting healthcare services and facilities in addition to regular tourist facilities" (Gooderich, 1991). An attempt by consumers to decrease the cost and waiting times of healthcare provision whilst still receiving qual-ity treatment is another perspective that explains the popularity of healthcare travel at least in part.

   The healthcare travel sector has been classified into three categories (Henderson, 2004):
1. Spas and alternative therapies – acupuncture, aroma - theraphy, beauty care, herbal healing, homeopathy, massage, meditation, yoga, and other general well-being treatments;
2. Cosmetic surgery – breast augmentation, facelifts, liposuction, and other non-essential medical procedures,

3. Medical travel – covering such medical services as health screening, heart surgeries, cancer treatment, joint replacements, and other surgical operations typically requiring hospitalization and professional healthcare.

More generally the healthcare travel sector can be classified in predictive (medical check ups), preventive (spas), perfective (cosmetic surgery) and acute (heart surgery) curing practices.

The travel aspect of healthcare travel can be interpreted as:

- A combination of curing and visiting a specific country for touristic purposes. This is appropriate for relative expensive but light treatments. The travel costs are offset, at least in part, by the decreased curing costs.
- A combination of curing and visiting a specific country for meeting family and friends. The visiting friends and relatives option is applicable for expats and people with roots in a specific country.

The combination of healthcare, travel and tourism seems to be very new, but this is not the case. In 18th and 19th century going to a spa in Europe was a well accepted method to cure form for numerous ailments (Connel, 2005). And it should be remembered that the cost in time needed to bridge travel distances were considerable; often much longer than contemporary long-haul air travel. In this article refers to "healthcare travel" rather than the term "healthcare tourism" or "medical tourism". Whilst touristic aspects may be involved, the term 'travel' is considered more appropriate in that it emphasizes the need to bridge geographical distance for healthcare purposes; whereas a potential touristic ad-on of a trip would be a secondary consideration.

Justifications for healthcare travel are to a significant extent economic in nature and most often have to do with issues of a lack of capacity or the high costs both in terms of time and fiscal expenditure. In particular the malfunctioning of the healthcare system in Western nations has resulted in:

- The motive amongst a growing number of patients from industrialized countries to travel to emerging nations for medical treatment;
- Rising awareness that the latter are capable of providing medical treatment at much lower costs and quicker than would be possible in the patient's home country;
- The emergence of a healthcare travel sector equipped to respond to the expanding demand in a dedicated manner, and;
- The need for a new literacy to address the issues that may arise in healthcare travel which involves two broad areas of expertise, healthcare and the travel trade, but which have been traditionally administered in isolation from one another. Their current merging needs to ap-

propriately addressed, so as to avoid potential contradictions and conflicts.

For the Netherlands healthcare travel is relative new. The most important
driver for using this concept was the waiting time for surgery in the Dutch
hospitals and the possibilities in Belgian and German hospitals. Some Dutch
care providers have already set up care provisions in Spain for elderly to get
their care and services while enjoying the climate. Insurers cover this care
under the same conditions as they apply in The Netherlands (Driest, 2006).
For not assured curing (cosmetic surgery, dental implantations, eye laser
treatment) destinations in Spain, Turkey and Asian countries like Thailand
and India are used, but no exact data are available. An indication can be derived by the results of a survey (Nivel, 2004):

- Of the Dutch population 35 percent is willing to go abroad for medical
  services
- Only 3 percent of the Dutch population has actually had the choice to
  travel abroad for healthcare.
- Two-thirds of this latter group did really travel abroad. Most of them
  did travel to Belgium (64 %) and to Germany.
- The report concludes that only few people ever used healthcare abroad
  but once people are given the choice the vast majority will choose to
  go abroad.

Although not explicitly stated, it is possible that respondents might not have
considered countries as far as India or Singapore but rather the neighbouring
countries while answering the NIVEL questionnaire.

The purpose of healthcare travel originating from the Netherlands seems
to have different motives in comparison to the UK experience. Out of a small
survey (47 respondents) was concluded that in the Dutch context a health
travel visit to a medical specialist (71,8 %) followed by surgery (12,8 %) was
the most important purpose (Nivel, 2005). Dental treatment contributed only
to 2,6 %. In contrast the results of a UK survey reveal that the UK in 2006
served as the origin for healthcare travel, particularly 22,000 dental patients
(43 %) and 14,500 cosmetic surgery patients (29 %) (Treatmentabroad,
2008). Relatively little is known about the behavior and intentions of healthcare travelers.

Healthcare travel can be a solution for the in section 2 described needs to
reduce costs and to increase availability of healthcare. It also can be a method
to increase the quality of care. In general healthcare travel is an example of
the in section 3 described changed perspective to a market-driven, individual-

ized and globalized healthcare. Some forms tend to more orientation to care instead of cure, to perfective and preventive curing. A very important driver for the first consumers is to overcome treatments that presently are not covered by patient's insurance. The motivations as recorded by the an International Passenger Survey in the UK reflects these motivations kilometres (Treatmentabroad, 2008).

4.2   Local Care: RP Care

RP Care is an innovative modular extension of Roompot Vacations, providing guests (both domestic and European Union) to obtain a variety of quality health and wellness services while also enjoying a Dutch sea and sand vacation. RP Care is an example of healthcare travel. RP Care has been established in part in response to the international focus of healthcare travel. The service has been created in an effort to address the demand noted by the number of Dutch, German and English travelers who are traveling abroad to avoid long waiting lines and/or electing to undertake elective medical procedures while on vacation. Roompot felt that it could expand on its initial entry into the healthcare, started five years ago with the offering of kidney dialysis at the Banjaard, a five-star holiday bungalow park, located 10 from the first Roompot Park established 40 years ago. The kidney dialysis service stemmed from the local hospital's inability to service the needs of an expanded vacation market. As a member of the local hospital board, the founder of Roompot was aware of both the need for additional dialysis service and the hospital's desire to establish an off-site clinic. Thus in true entrepreneurial spirit, a separate building was constructed within the park to house the dialysis service. Patients no longer had to travel to and remain in a hospital for the procedure. Rather they have the option of visiting the clinic three times a week, for 2 weeks, enjoying a non-sterile, relaxed but professional environment. Appointments can be made on line through the Roompot Vacations website, with the knowledge that the onsite medical staff are all associated with the local hospital.

Exhibit 2 outlines the modular services and amenities planned for various Roompot locations within Zeeland in partnership with local health providers. A clinic specializing in plastic surgery will be located in Goes, centrally positioned close to other Roompot parks and the regional hospital. Such a location is of benefit to both doctors and patients, who will be able to convalesce in a quality holiday setting, with family and/or friends.

The strategy to focus initially on the province of Zeeland is based in part on local knowledge of healthcare providers, networks and also represents the location of Roompot's base of operations. The strategy can be expanded into other provinces within Holland, based on local success and the learning curve.

Recreation	Cure	Care
Fun stuff	**Traditional:**	Nursing
Conference facilities	Cosmetic surgery	Nutrition
Pools	Orthopedic	Hospitality
Sauna	Optometry	
	Pain reduction	
	Radiology	
	X-rays	
	Physiotherapy	
	New:	
	Preventative	
	Acupuncture	

Figure 2: RP Care building blocks

In summary, we view RP Care as an example of a healthcare travel practice that:

- Offers a solution to the needs as described in section 2. It decreases cost to provide the medical services outside a hospital, increases the quality of caring and reduces waiting times
- Reflects the changed perspective as described in section 3 towards market-driven, individualized, regionalized and care orientated solutions.

4.3 Cure and Care Cooperation: The Case of India

For some time, patients originating in United States and England have journeyed to India for a specific treatment. Excellent care coupled with English language proficiency makes also the Netherlands an interesting market, especially its large Hindustani and Indian population for Indian healthcare travel (Lai et al, 2006). As result of a survey was concluded that 25 % of the inhabitants of The Netherlands who are People of Indian Origin and other people with ties to India do have a very positive attitude for going to India for Healthcare purposes (NS BPi, 2007). As Connell stated: "India is capitalizing on its low costs and highly trained doctors to appeal to these 'medical tourists.' Even with airfare, the cost of going to India for surgery can be markedly cheaper, and the quality of services is often better than that found in the

United States and UK. Indeed, many patients are pleased at the prospect of combining their tummy tucks with a trip to the Taj Mahal." (Connell, 2005)

Indian healthcare travel is another specific example of the description of the concept of healthcare travel in section 4.1. In fact it may be viewed as an extrapolation of this concept in the Dutch healthcare market context. Particularly when one considers that:

- The geographical distance between India and The Netherlands is much more significant than between the Netherlands and Belgium presently the most visited health travel destination for patients who originate from the Netherlands.
- The awareness of the possibilities of Indian healthcare for patients who originate from the Netherlands is very low; in the western world there is a dominant stereotype that the healthcare facilities in India are undeveloped (Connell, 2005).
- The availability of healthcare facilities of high quality in India is much larger than the actual health care demand in the Netherlands.

Resourcing the option of healthcare travel affords both Indian and Dutch stakeholders opportunities to grow from idea through developmental and testing stages to the implementation stage of Innovation. The application of new product and process innovation would afford healthcare providers to offer better care, more quickly at lower costs. In the domain of process innovation transnational healthcare cooperation would enable the transfer of clinical research and diagnostics performed in India to the medical specialists in the Netherlands. In this instance, the medical records would do the travelling, whereas the Dutch patients can remain in the Netherlands.

On a research and development level there are technology transfer opportunities to capitalize on, enabling Indian healthcare specialists to access know-how from Dutch medical specialists treatments as of yet, unavailable in India. For instance, Dutch medical specialists have build a strong reputation in "Targeted treatment", Oncology, Bio-Informatics and Patient Registrations Systems. In addition collaborations between India and the Netherlands can lead to affordable and accessible high quality medical care that would benefit India's low-income groups. Finally, the field of training through exchanges of, for example, medical students and nurses presents ample opportunity for cooperation between India and The Netherlands is furthermore potential to achieve synergistic effects.

Healthcare cooperation between The Netherlands and India can be a solution for the in section 2 described needs to reduce costs and waiting times and even raise the quality level for The Netherlands and to increase availability of healthcare for India. In general healthcare cooperation is an example of the changed perspective to a market-driven, individualized and globalized healthcare described in section 3. Due to the distance, both geographical and cultural, between The Netherlands and India the option of treatment and technology transfer represents a viable option, particularly through the management of virtual projects and help reduce the need to travel, where appropriate.

5   Levers for Implementing Novel Healthcare Concepts
Section 4 described healthcare travel solutions. To implement these novel concepts to their full potential several underlying needs arise in the Dutch healthcare market that are addressed in this section. These needs are categorised under for sub-headings: information, quality, integration and care for the environment.

5.1   Information
To improve transparency as described in section 3 more information has to be available on the individual level. On the demand side of the market knowledge is needed to respond to questions such as:
- Who (healthcare provider) can provide what type of cure and care, where for whom?
- What are the costs for a specific cure and care option including travel, room and board?
- What are the estimated lead times (for waiting, travelling, staying in hospital, recovering near hospital, total recovery) involved in a particular health care treatment?
- What is the quality of a healthcare provider and how is this evidenced (e.g., by international accreditation and/ or testimonials)?
- What is insured in a care and cure process and under which conditions?

On the supply side of the market knowledge is needed about matters such as:
- The expected volume per treatment
- The expected cure / care quality by the consumers
- Ways to find and approach customers.

On the level of interaction between a patient and a specific healthcare provider or physician knowledge can contribute to:

- Identifying an optimal means to get acquainted to each other (traditionally done by a first visit)
- Determining without hassle, i.e., without doing unnecessary fact finding (as blood and X-ray diagnosis) so that precious time can be spend on diagnosis of the actual medical situation and the patient's history;
- Reaching agreement which knowledge is vital or non-vital and dynamic or non-dynamic. In a best possible scenario only the vital dynamic information has to be generated again. But nowadays in healthcare, doctors, hospitals and research institutions generally maintain strict control over what many view as proprietary information. That barrier needs to be bridged to arrive at a patient-centric treatment system (IBM, 2004).

5.2 Quality Management

Internationalized standardized quality management is needed to answer what is perhaps the most urgent of questions in a patient's mind: "How do I know if a hospital and /or physician is competent? What to do in case of treatment failure?"With the possibility to choose individually the need has risen for assurance that the right choice will be made. In order to pre-empt such patient worries healthcare providers need:

- Internal quality systems at hospitals that can be audited by independent auditors
- Accreditation by government, insurance companies and / or independent bodies
- Development and acceptance of an international healthcare quality system. The global use of the ISO norm for healthcare will improve transparency of the market and herewith support individualization and globalization
- A system of conflict resolution at the consulted healthcare provider. Unless which quality system is used and the intrinsic quality of a healthcare provider, conflicts about the healthcare service and the outcome of this service ("I am not cured!") can occur. To increase trust for the healthcare consumer and provider at each provider a system of conflict resolution has to exist. Specific needs are:
  - o Rights for both parties
  - o Ways to resolve complaints
  - o Ways to escalate the conflict to independent parties in case of conflicts.

5.3 Integration

As accustomed in the local hospital the new healthcare consumer expects global healthcare "integrators". Those integrators provide the total process of curing and caring: pre care, travel, curing and after care. Not only for the patient but also for its direct environment (spouse, parents, children) if needed. Those providers also have to insure second order risks (illness during the trip, complications etc.) of healthcare travelling.

5.4 Environment

To respond to unintended effects, healthcare travel providers must be ready to answer to any possible negative media portrayals, including challenges concerned with environmental and ethical effects of novel care and cure concepts. For instance:

- To what extent may increased (air) travel consequent to global care contribute to global warming?
- To what extent may the care provision to people originating in developed countries result in a possible care shortage for patients in less developed countries?
- To what extent may global best in class healthcare provision contribute to the expansion of social exclusion?

6 Novel Concept Enablers

To implement the new healthcare travel concepts as described in section 4 enabling innovations are needed. These innovations cope with the needs as described in section 5. The concepts described in this concluding section represent some examples of the role that relative small innovations can play in contributing to transforming the overall healthcare system.

6.1 Individual Ownership Over Medical Information

Due to the need of individual ownership over medical information the next already existing concepts can be used:

- Medstick - The Medstick is a completely electronic mobile medical database on a USB stick. The Medstick consists all the medical information of the owner of the stick (Cinsol). The main advantage is that people who frequently travel, people who have a high medical risk, older people, people with high-risk jobs etc., always have their medical file at hand in case they use more healthcare providers or there is an emergency. Other solutions for storing individual health information could be the use of websites like Google Health (Google).

- Testimonials – Testimonials of cured patients provided on paper or via internet can inform and convince new users of new concepts.

6.2 Virtualization of Contact

The actual existing information and communication technology enables virtualization of the healthcare provider and healthcare consumer encounter. Specific possible concepts to support such vital encounters include:

- Websites to provide information – Websites as Webmd (Webmd) provide information about the quality of hospitals and physicians to help individuals with their specific choice. In The Netherlands Independer (Indpender) provides such information about the Dutch supply side and under development is a website devoted to "Innovative Healthcare Collaborations with India". It will serve as an interface between the Netherlands and India in the field of healthcare Innovation & collaboration (NFBPI).
- The virtualization of a visit to a physician – To reduce physical contact moments with physicians visits can be virtualised. This will need new software to schedule and make appointments happen with the needed security and confidentiality.
- The virtualization of visits by friends and relatives in the hospital – When the location of hospital is not in the neighborhood physical visits will be restricted to few people. The use of internet can solve this problem by making such visits virtual.

6.3 Insure Specific Situations

With the increasing individualization the need for specific insurance policies rises. As an example in the Netherlands the Insurance company Azivo has announced a Suriname policy (Azivo). In this insurance policy specific preventive care and curing facilities in Suriname is insured. Other policies that can be developed:

- International insurance policy – for people who want always best in class healthcare
- Preventive insurance policy – for people who want often medical check ups and act upon the given advice
- India insurance policy – for people who accept curing in India in case use of Indian hospitals provide overall cost reduction.

6.4   Healthcare Travel Integrators

As discussed in section 6 the new healthcare consumer expects in the global healthcare "integrators". The most likely and trusted integrator will be the local hospital who take the role of "front office" and propose and organize the total process of curing and caring by selected "back offices" which can be anywhere. Alternative integrators are insurance companies and travel agencies. At present several small travel agencies provide healthcare opportunities directed at Indian and Dutch consumers.

7   Conclusion

There is an urgent need for innovating care and cure in The Netherlands. Healthcare has to be provided better, faster and affordable. Fortunately the innovation of healthcare is stimulated by changing perspectives (as market-orientation, individualization, globalization and virtualization).

The described healthcare travel concepts correspond with these changing perspectives and will change the healthcare system in the Netherlands as we now know it. Implementation of these concepts will have long implementation times because the perceived discontinuity with traditional provided healthcare which still reflect the old perspectives (as public-regulated, group oriented, localized and always face-to-face meetings). This paradigm shift will take time and will introduce new champions who understand and can manage the new field of play.

The paradox between the need of well insured, integrated and standardized curing and a customer centric care has to be solved by new concepts to provide information, to manage quality and to organise cure and care. Also the care for the environment is a constraint for implementing new concepts. Relative small innovations can contribute in these areas to transform the overall healthcare system. Expected is that these innovations will have their own reason for existence and therefore can be introduced independently as is illustrated by some already existing solutions. They will contribute to a new healthcare system where travelling for curing accompanied by virtual contact with the physician (before and after) and relatives (during) will be normal reflecting the individual needs and wishes.

References

Azivo, http://www.azivo.nl/index.php?pageId=36&newsId=56
Christensen, C (1997), The Innovator's Dilemma, Boston, Harvard Business School Press.
Cinsol, http://www.cinsol.nl/

Connel (2005), Medical tourism: Sea, sun, sand and surgery, in: Tourism Management 27 (2006), pp. 1093–1100.

Consortium Sneller Beter pijler 3, Sneller Beter werkt! Resultaten van het eerste jaar, June, 2006 Scheepsbouwer, Zorg voor innovatie, Sneller Beter- Innovatie en ICT in de curatieve zorg. Eindrapportage KPN, 2006.

CPB, Verplaatsing vanuit Nederland, Februar 2005.

Driest, P. (2006), Long-term care in Europe, in: Farming for Health, J. Hassink and M. van Dijk (eds.), pp. 101–106. Netherlands: Springer.

Gooderich, J. and Gooderich, G. (1991), Health Care Tourism, in: Medlik, S. (ed.) Managing Tourism, Oxford: Butterworth-Heinemann, pp. 107–114.

Google, http://www.google.com/intl/nl/health/tour/index.html

Henderson, J. (2004), Healthcare Tourism in Southeast Asia, in: Tourism Review International, 7(3/4) pp. 111–121.

IBM, (2004), Global Innovation Outlook, 2004, Retrieved May 9, 2006 page 23, http://domino.watson.ibm.com/comm/www_innovate.nsf/images/gio/$FILE/IBM_GIO_2004.pdf.

Independer, http://www.independer.nl/gezondheidszorg/VVZiekenhuizen.aspx.

Lai, P.Y., Mandemaker P., Goel K., Healthcare tourism to India, Matching Dutch healthcare demand and Indian healthcare supply, 2006.

NFBPI, www.nfbpi.nl.

NIVEL, E. van der Schee, D.M.J. Delnoij, Voor zorg naar het buitenland: veel mensen willen het, weinigen doen het, 2004.

NS BPi, Marktonderzoek Medisch Toerisme naar India, Wahid Saleh. Deepraj Das, Ronald Israels, Peter Gobets, Piter Mandemaker, 2007.

O'Neil,E. www.futurehealth.ucsf.edu/pdf_files/Long %20Beach %20AAHP %204-11.ppt.

Shimo, A. (2006), Private Care in Canada, in: Macleans, Vol. 119, No.18, pp 31–53.

SCP, SCP-publicatie 2007/31, Verklaringsmodel verpleging en verzorging 2007, Jedid-Jah Jonker, Klarita Sadiraj, Isolde Woittiez, Michiel Ras, Meike Morren, Den Haag, Sociaal en Cultureel Planbureau, november 2007.

The Wall Street Journal, October 17-19 2008, pp. 14–15.

Tidd, J., Bessant, J., & Pavitt, K (2000), Managing Innovation Integrating Technological, Market and Organizational Change, 2nd ed., Chicester: Wiley.

Treatmentabroad (2008), Medical Tourism Fact Sheet, www.treatmentabroad.com.

Ueng, Grace Whi-Tze (2006), Globalization Of Healthcare: The World Is Getting Flatter; Economic Opportunities Beckon, http://localtechwire.com/business/local_tech_wire/opinion/ story/1167955/, Posted: Aug 28, 2006.

Webmd, http://hospital.webmd.com/index.aspx?f=webmd1bha3504.

Wikipedia, http://en.wikipedia.org/wiki/Medical_tourism, 2008, October 18th.

GRZEGORZ GOLEMBSKI AND MARCIN OLSZEWSKI

The Spas of Salt Mine Bochnia – A Polish Case Study

Poland has recently embarked on a fast track of economic growth. This growth, however, started from a low base and in early stages developed in the conditions of an almost universal state ownership. Changes in the economy over the last eighteen years (1990–2008) have been very dynamic and made a great impact on the tourism industry.

Privatisation processes – the core of economic reform in Poland – have been particularly intensive in the tourism sector. Enterprises which belonged to the private sector before 1989 were mostly sold to private investors and new set up ones are private. Today over 95 % of all travel agencies and hospitality companies are privately owned. The rate of investment in the tourism industry is also very high. This is evidenced by a rapid growth in the availability of bed-places in hotels – from 50 thousand in 1990 to 134 thousand in 2006.

The opening of borders, introduction of low-cost airlines, relative decline of prices for tourism services, and the growing intensity of marketing have all contributed to a dynamic growth of international tourism in Poland. In 2007 the revenue from inbound tourism amounted to USD 10.6 billion.

International tourism is concentrated mainly in the large cities. Asked about the reasons for limiting their offerings respondents usually cite conservative marketing invariably aimed at traditional market segments, inadequate transportation infrastructure (poor road network), and shortage of alternative products.

With enhanced tourism products increasingly coming to the market this state of affairs is now being changed and the effects are already apparent. This is consistent with global trends, such as:

- A clear tendency to seek new ways of satisfying tourism needs. Traditional forms of tourism development are increasingly being criticised and efforts are made to integrate tourism with social values (W.L. Smith, W.R. Eadington, 1995). Customisation of tourism offerings is growing in importance, and innovative service packages are being put together (A. Niezgoda, P. Zmyślony 2003, p. 204). Short breaks are now more in demand (S. Briggs, 2001, p. 38). Traditional tourism based on the "3 S" formula (sea, sand, sun) is being replaced with the "3 E" tourism (entertainment, excitement, education; W. Alejziak, 1999, p. 213)

- Exploration of new opportunities to develop products aimed at education and knowledge-based tourism, nature-based (eco-) tourism, and health improvement.

In order to achieve a market success and be economically viable, a tourism product must be addressed to a broadest possible range of market segments. Such a policy is likely to result in increased visitation, longer stays, and subsequently more revenue from selling tourism goods and services. It also provides a unique opportunity for releasing local initiative (in local governments and individuals), ultimately creating wealth for the region. This can be achieved through entrepreneurship and innovation.

According to Drucker, entrepreneurship is about creating new consumer satisfaction and/or generating new consumer demand. Hence entrepreneurial activities are centred on searching for opportunities in the market and creating new resources to take advantage of these opportunities. Entrepreneurship is also a process whereby individuals look for opportunities regardless of the resources that may or may not be in their possession (H.H. Stevenson, J. C. Jarillo, 1990, p. 23). Consequently, entrepreneurial activities are performed in conditions of uncertainty, and are burdened with risk. Changes that take place around tourism firms require the management of those firms to monitor the changing environment, react immediately or even anticipate the change.

While there is no entrepreneurship without a new concept, nore does it exist if the new concept is not being consistently implemented (T.T. Tkaczyk et al., 2000, p. 80). Entrepreneurship in tourism is about changing the rules of market play and moving away from stereotypical perception of tourism products. It requires creativity in satisfying the needs and wants of tourists. The aim is to make a company's product positively distinct in the eyes of the consumer.

Innovation is the tool used by entrepreneurs to convert a change into an opportunity by starting a new business venture or providing a new service (P. F. Drucker, p. 29). Entrepreneurship is thus the precondition for innovation (J. Mattsson, J. Sundbo, Ch. Fussing-Jenes, 2000). The entrepreneur creates the innovative spirit and the necessary structures, procures the knowledge and capital (J. Mattsson, J. Sundbo, Ch. Fussing-Jenes, 2000). A change in a company or an organisation becomes an innovation of a proper scale only when and if it has been accepted by relevant stakeholders and cast in the form of standard practices, procedures, and/or products (W. Świtalski, 2005, p. 68). Services can be innovative in two ways (J. Gadrey, F. Gallouj, O. Weinstein, 1995):

1. Through organising the solution of a new problem. New problems may be formulated by clients or "created" by innovative service providers anticipating changes in demand through interaction between the service provider and the client.
2. Through organising a more efficient way of solving problems which are already known (changing the methods, processes, technical systems, etc).

The aim of the present analysis is to identify characteristics of a company that place it among entrepreneurial innovators. In our selection of the case for analysing entrepreneurial and innovative behaviours within the IEN project we accepted a proposition put forward by the Polish Agency for Tourism Development who suggested The Spas of Salt Mine Bochnia as an interesting object of investigation.

The Spas of Salt Mine Bochnia was established in 1995 as a public company wholly owned by the State Treasury. Its stated business was the exploitation of an old salt mine, defunct since 1990, for tourism. In its initial stage of existence (1995–2002) the company performed the necessary adaptations of the underground facilities to make them available for tourists. By the end of 2001 the firm known as "The Spas of Salt Mine Bochnia" was privatised. Following the handover of the company control to private ownership, development of the facility accelerated with a view to adjust the product to market requirements and fully utilise the opportunities inherent in the site. At present the equity capital of the company amounts to PLN 4.229 million (EUR 1.5 m) with 70 % of company shares belonging to a private investor and the balance remaining in the possession of the state owned company Bochnia Salt Mine in liquidation. A private entrepreneur who was not connected with tourism so far (but mainly with telecommunication) decided to diversify his business and become engaged in tourism, perceiving it as a very profitable one. By contract the company leases from the state underground tunnels and chambers, the recently reconstructed and modernised shafts: Sutoris and Campi, as well as a miniature underground train for transporting tourists. The Spas of Salt Mine Bochnia is the exclusive leaseholder of the present and future underground tunnels and rooms of the salt mine adapted to tourism.

Developments that have taken place in the salt mine since the handover of the facility to private operators can be characterised as innovative. The new owners asked themselves the question: what needs can be created with such a valuable asset as the salt mine and how can these needs be satisfied? The follow-up questions were suggested by the tourists themselves who reported their needs after having visited the facility, and concerned specific solutions for satisfying those extra needs in a novel way.

To gauge the innovativeness of the company's offering we need to analyse the product structure, i.e. identify its core benefits, elements of the tangible product (conceptualisation of the product core), and elements of the augmented product (product differentiation in the target market).

The product core are the benefits derived by tourists from the unique ambience of the underground tunnels and chambers of the salt mine and its specific, healthy microclimate. These benefits include adventure, fun, recreation, relaxation, health improvement and the like.

A skilful conceptualisation of the product core served as the basis for subsequent adaptation works in the salt mine and the provision of hotel, catering, recreational and health facilities, both underground and over ground.

Established in 1248, Bochnia is the oldest salt mine in Poland and at the same time the oldest European salt extraction enterprise. After almost eight centuries of excavations, the salt mine in Bochnia is like a vast underground town abounding in mysterious, extraordinary places. Located in close proximity to the 12th century shaft of the salt mine, Sutoris Hotel provides accommodation in single, double and triple bedrooms, studios and a suite. All rooms have en suite bathrooms, satellite television, telephone, and broadband access to internet. With two conference rooms (housing 35 and 100 persons respectively) furnished with audiovisual equipment the hotel offers full service in organising conferences and training sessions. The décor of the hotel's Grota restaurant alludes to the history of the salt mine. The chef prepares for his guests traditional miners' dishes as well as Polish and European cuisine.

In 1996 The Spas of Salt Mine Bochnia formally registered as a health care facility and secured a contract with the National Health Authority to provide health services in the salt mine. Outpatient surgeries and the Rehabilitation and Biological Regeneration Centre located in the hotel offer a wide range of treatments such as Jacuzzi and whirlpool baths, salt baths, hot and cold water jets ("Scottish water whips"), whirlpool massages of upper and lower limbs, vacuum massages, laser therapy, phototherapy, heat therapy, magneto therapy, electrotherapy, kinezy therapy, and inhalations.

The innovative character of the product offered by Salt Mine Bochnia lies in the range of services making up the product. A defunct salt mine has been turned into an attraction supported by services hitherto not proposed to tourists. This project satisfies the necessary condition of entrepreneurship which states that the innovative entrepreneur introduces totally irregular changes, upsets the existing balance, smashes the old habits and ultimately creates a new equilibrium and a new market (T.T. Tkaczyk et al., 2000, p. 72). The range of services offered by the company goes beyond the traditional scope of attractions attributable to salt mines anywhere. The company's main competitor, the nearby Wieliczka Salt Mine, offers sightseeing routes in the underground tunnels and chambers but is less concerned about its above ground facilities. With its service offer targeted at a different market segment, The Spas of Salt Mine Bochnia has created a new market attracting consumers hitherto not interested in salt mines. As an innovator-leader Salt Mine Bochnia is the only tourism accommodation establishment in Poland offering subterranean dwelling facilities. The range of health improvement services offered by the company is also unique as natural subterranean therapy is possible only in two locations in Poland. A feature that distinguishes Bochnia among other projects of this type is a great emphasis placed on its above-ground facilities. The underlying idea of developing the product known as "The Spas of Salt Mine Bochnia" was to attract a hitherto unexplored segment of the market by exploiting a defunct salt mine in an unconventional way. A decision was made to offer services to consumers who might not otherwise be interested in subterranean tourism and who remain outside the interest of Bochnia's main competitor, i.e. Wieliczka Salt Mine.

Generally, Salt Mine Bochnia targets three types of clients: individual, institutional, and school parties. Individual clients can choose therapeutic stays of different duration in underground salt chambers where treatment is offered for such ailments as allergies, respiratory conditions, and asthma. This segment of clients is also offered short breaks including weekend and public holiday stays, and sightseeing trips. The proposition for institutional clients includes staff integration programs, conferences, training sessions, events and parties. And finally, for the important segment of school parties the company has propositions such as overnight stays in the salt mine, "green school" programs, summer and winter camps, and special themed tours of underground tunnels of the salt mine.

Tourists can choose between one of the two guided tour routes: the tourist route or the geological route. The tourist route takes about 1.5–2 hours to walk. The extreme combination of tourist and geological routes requires some physical fitness. The routes start from the oldest level of the salt mine dating back to the 13th century and proceed through a network of old passages, crosscuts, and rooms. Since 2008 a new attraction is available. It is a subterranean boat trip 230 meters underground.

The company's main objective is to extend the duration of stays rather than increase the number of visitors. This goal has already been achieved by expansion of aboveground facilities and developing a product attractive enough to make tourists stay longer and to use a wide range of available services.

Longer duration of stays has also been achieved thanks to the availability of underground accommodation facilities. The company adapted two underground chambers to provide overnight dwellings for tourists. The larger of the two, the Wazyn Chamber located 250 metres underground, provides 300 bed-places and also houses a gymnasium, movie theatre, and "Wazynek" restaurant. The other one, offering a higher standard – the Koldras Chamber – provides accommodation in two-, three-, and four–bed cubicles, where each bed has its own bedside lamp and a pushbutton to ring a bell in the nurse room if a guest requires assistance of a night duty nurse.

A night in the salt mine is not just fun. This is also a recognised therapy to treat such ailments as asthma, chronic sinusitis or pollen allergy. So an overnight stay combines great fun with health improving inhalations. Year after year this service is growing in popularity.

"The Spas of Salt Mine Bochnia" product has been developed with the aim to attract a hitherto unexplored segment of the market by exploiting a salt mine in a way that nobody had thought of before. The Spas of Salt Mine Bochnia is an example of a creative imitation strategy postulated by Drucker. In this strategy an entrepreneur creatively develops an already existing idea and does it better than those who were first to use it because as an entrepreneur he/she better understands the nature of innovation (P. Drucker, p. 239). Having identified its target segments the company must find ways of reaching the potential client with its message. At present the company directs its message to domestic customers, but it has plans to expand to international markets. The company's website contains information about products targeted directly at the three identified segments. The offers are publicised in three separate types of product catalogues, brochures, and price lists, meant for distribution in the respective market segments. Advertising is affected through internet commercial websites, local press, radio, as well as specialized periodic publications (business and medical). Promotional materials are also sent directly to medical practitioners and school teachers. In addition, the company sponsors medical conferences. The sales network is based on tourist agencies, and a network of school teachers and medical practitioners. To sum, the innovative character of the company is expressed in the following:

1. The product core is consistent with the current trends in consumer demand (adventure, recreation, health improvement);
2. The way of satisfying consumer needs is different from what is being offered in the market, and places the company among the leaders of innovation;
3. A wide range of services available both underground and on the surface makes the site even more attractive;
4. The product combines anthropogenic elements (the oldest salt mine), with natural features (microclimate), health improvement (recreation and sport facilities), entertainment and education.
5. Using the central element of the product – the salt mine – the company put together an offer which is attractive enough to make tourists stay much longer than they do in the competing salt mine in Wieliczka, and spend a lot more money;
6. Longer stays of tourists provide an impulse for local infrastructure development and an opportunity for the local community and entrepreneurs, thus widening the possibilities for growth in the whole region.

The company continues in its efforts to develop the innovative element of the product. The underlying theme is to further enhance and differentiate the offer, and to improve logistics of the product. The product has been extended to include the salt mine industrial facilities located on the surface around of the Campi shaft about 1.5 kilometres from the main entrance to the mine, in the town centre. The following actions have been taken to enhance the product:
- the old brine graduation tower is being reconstructed and will be made available for sightseeing;
- an observation deck is going to be opened to the public on top of the existing chimney;
- the old salt works buildings are being adapted to the needs of the sanatorium;
- an open-air exhibition of old mining equipment has been put together on the grounds of the salt mine.

On the other hand, the product's logistics need improvement in the area of transporting tourists between the entrance and the exit of the salt mine's underground facilities (visitors enter the salt mine in the town centre and exit some distance away from the main entrance, in an area where cars and coaches can be parked). In developing a tourism product it is important to look at it as a complete whole. A well-organised product core may not be enough if attention is not given to the details of the tangible product and its surroundings. The tangible product attributes include features and services that make a visit more attractive and cause tourists to stay longer (accommodation, food, local culture and folklore, access, signposting, tourist information, car parks, guiding services). By the product surroundings we understand such elements as technical infrastructure, natural environment, population ratios, investment possibilities (ownership structure, land use zoning), transportation infrastructure.

A development gap between the product core on the one hand and the tangible product and its surroundings on the other can be detrimental for the viability of investment. Hence it is purposeful to look at the basic stimulants and impediments in the development of the tangible product and its surroundings. The tangible product is shaped by many actors: the firm responsible for the product core, local and regional governments, and service providers and their professional associations (accommodation and food serving establishments, shop owners, owners of recreation facilities, organisers of cultural and folklore events). Relations between those entities are key to the quantitative and qualitative development of the tangible product.

1. Local (regional) governments impact on the tangible product through creating the general conditions for its development and through collaboration on specific projects. In the case of the The Spas of Salt Mine Bochnia examples of the general conditions include:

STIMULANTS
Town development strategy in which tourism is identified as the leading development factor. Implementation of the strategy resulted in the drafting of 22 zoning plans (at a cost of EUR 1 million). The zoning will enable fast processing of building permissions which will result in less delay in the construction of facilities enhancing the tangible product (hotels, access roads); Steps are taken by local authorities to include Bochnia salt mine on UNESCO's World Heritage List. Such listing would contribute to more investment in tourism and a faster completion of tourism projects. The investment climate will be further improved if:

- the salt mine is awarded the status of a spa (only the underground facilities are considered); however, efforts made by the local authorities in this regard have met
- with considerable resistance from the spa lobby which argue that a spa may only be located in an administrative division (commune) which itself has a spa status as a whole (that is, it must be set in appropriate natural environment);

- the plans for constructing a nearby motorway will include an exit road connecting the motorway with the town of Bochnia. Given the 40 kilometer distance from Cracow by motorway, this is a key issue for increasing tourism flows to Bochnia. Talks are in progress at the voivodship level (the highest administrative division in Poland).

The efforts to provide favourable general conditions for tourism development have already resulted in the removal of bureaucratic barriers delaying the completion of specific projects. This problem particularly concerned access roads and new tourist accommodation and service establishments in the town centre (the Campi shaft area). Further, the local government issued permission for the erection of large welcoming billboards informing about the product on municipal land.

IMPEDIMENTS
- Development of the product is seriously hampered by lack of space for the construction of car parks. The main entrance to the salt mine facilities is situated in the town centre where there is no room for new surface car parks. On the other hand, construction of underground or multi-storey car parks is beyond financial means of both the company and local government.
- Another impediment arises from municipal plans competing with the salt mine project. The town is planning to build a large industrial park (benign to the environment) on the outskirts near the planned motorway exit. These plans exemplify a conflict of interest between the partners. The local government apparently sees more benefit in the development of its own assets than from an already existing product which the town does not own.

2. Actions of the local government aimed at providing favourable general conditions for the specific tourism product are also beneficial to other service providers in town. Investors find it easier to obtain building permissions, and in the running of their businesses benefit from other incentives provided by the local authorities, such as:

STIMULANTS
- Preferential tax rates for all hotels operating in town.
- Free of charge training for small enterprises (mainly VAT and other taxation issues)

143

- Tax reduction for those who invest their own money in the renovation of building facades, thus improving the general impression of the town.

By contrast, IMPEDIMENTS include:
- Under-representation of service providers in business associations or other professional bodies and non-governmental organisations. It makes it difficult for the local people to participate in the promotion of local culture and hampers the efforts to develop a planned policy for tourism services provision. This situation is characteristic of young democracies that emerged after a long spell of totalitarian rule in which citizens' initiatives were stifled.
- In the absence of informal network communications between the owner of the product core and small co-producers of the tangible product (shop owners, food outlets, and entertainment organisers) is inadequate. This gives the impression of a chaos in the provision of services. On the other hand, collaboration between The Spas of Salt Mine Bochnia (product core) and larger hotels is proceeding well, especially during high season.

In Poland the business surroundings play a particularly significant role. This is partly due to the enormous negative legacy left by the centrally-planned economy of a not so-distant past. This legacy concerns underdeveloped technical and transportation infrastructure, the natural environment, employment structures and many other aspects. All these elements impact on the business environment surrounding the product core. The shaping of business surroundings is also a responsibility of local governments. In the analysed case we were able to identify both pro-development factors (stimulants) and hampering factors (impediments):

STIMULANTS

Poland's accession to the European Union (May 2004) has resulted in an increased rate of infrastructure investments. During the last two years the town of Bochnia (population: 28 thousand) has spent EUR 50 million of EU structural funds to modernise its water and sewage network and build a water purification plant. Over the last seven years the town has added 100 km of new sewage pipes. Every year (2004, 2005, 2006) EUR 5 million of EU funds are being spent on roads and pavements in town. All this has improved the living conditions in Bochnia and contributes to lower costs of tourism investments.

A very promising development is a planned extension of the Balice Airport - Cracow fast train line to reach Wieliczka and Bochnia. It would provide a fast and direct access from the airport to Bochnia (45 minute travel).

IMPEDIMENTS

In a country showing (in the end of 2007) 11.4 % unemployment (7,4 % in Bochnia) it is an absolute paradox that one of the biggest problems hampering tourism development is shortage of labour. In Bochnia itself the shortage of labour is due to many factors of which the most important is labour migration from small towns to big cities (Cracow is only 40 kilometres away). Another problem is the migration of young educated people abroad. There is also a shortage of local education institutions preparing students for employment in the tourism sector (the local college does not teach the kind of skills required in tourism-related jobs). Local wages are still very low (in the range of EUR 300–350 per month in front-line positions), and will have to be raised to attract labour, which in turn could undermine the viability of certain investment projects.

Among the many hampering factors is also a high cost of electric power services, affecting street lighting in particular. This is due to a monopolistic position of the local power distribution company which is also responsible for maintaining and servicing the street lighting facilities.

And finally, faster development is hampered by a frustrating bureaucracy connected with the distribution of EU funds such as convergence funds. Applications for subsidies are checked and corrected a dozen-or-so times at different levels causing considerable delays in the transfer of money to the applicants, wasting investors' precious time and raising costs of investment projects.

It seems that ultimate success is contingent on the perception of tourism as a stimulating force in the development of the whole region. This, however, requires a change in attitude on the part of many actors involved in the tourism product development, including local authorities and the local community. These changes are in fact happening and will accelerate when people begin to notice the positive influence of the product on the development of the whole region. The positive influence is already apparent in:

Increased employment in The Spas of Salt Mine Bochnia itself and in services supporting the company's product. The company employs 81 people (52 female and 29 male), of whom 42 % have a higher education degree. Tour guiding services are contracted out to a group of about 100 self-employed individuals. The town statistics show that the number of retail outlets, restaurants and bars in direct proximity of the salt mine is growing fast.

Those located within the 300 metre radius from the salt mine already employ about 250 people.

Improved tourism infrastructure. Ten years ago, Bochnia with a population of 28 thousand did not have a hotel. Today, apart from two hotels owned by the salt mine, there are three other hotels with a total of 250 bed-places, employing about 100 extra people (three-star Millennium Hotel – 160 bed-places, three-star Colt Hotel – 50 bed-places, and two-star Zalesie Hotel – 40 bed-places). The growing number of visitors has been an argument supporting the decision to build a swimming pool in town three years ago.

The aim of every entrepreneurial action is improvement of economic performance. In the studied case the project was initiated only in 2001, and since then the company invested over EUR 8.5 million in the venture. The effects of investments are usually not evident until several years after (in early stages of a company's existence sales are relatively low while operating costs and the cost of debt servicing are high). The analyzed data show established, systematical economic outcome improvement in the company. It concerns income and expense dynamism as well as profit and loss account. This is apparent in the following short analysis of company results:

Rate of sales growth, 2002 = 100

Years	2002	2003	2004	2005	2006	2007
SALES	100	143	198	240	254	318

Comment: sales are growing very fast.

Rate of costs growth, 2002 = 100

Years	2002	2003	2004	2005	2006	2007
COSTS	100	152	190	210	189	237

Comment: the rate of sales growth is greater than the cost increases.

The most important fact is that since 2003 the dynamism of loss is systematically decreasing, moreover since 2007 the enterprise makes a profit on the business.

Rate of loss generation, 2002 = 100

Years	2002	2003	2004	2005	2006	2007
COMPANY LOSSES	100	221	113	12	5	-3

Against the background of the above analysis of the product and the company's performance we might ask the question: What are the major barriers to entrepreneurship as seen by the company itself? In the company management's opinion the barriers mainly reside in the business surroundings beyond the company's control. As these barriers are characteristic of economies undergoing transformation from centrally planned systems to market economies, they must be looked at in more detail. The company operates in a permanent legal uncertainty arising from the fact, that the salt mine in liquidation is still a state-owned company, and effectively the state owns 30 % of the Spas of Salt Mine Bochnia. This has the following implications:

1. In countries undergoing transformation from centrally planned to market economies, usually starting from an almost 100 % state ownership of factors of production, privatisation progress and state assets management are often dependant on the attitudes of subsequent governments. It seems to be a rule that the more populist and nationalistic a government, the slower the rate of privatisation and the business sector encounters more problems in procuring or controlling assets of liquidated state companies. If the state is a partner in a private sector venture and its decisions become unpredictable, innovative actions are burdened with greater risk. This problem is equally widespread at the central level (such as in the case of The Spas of Salt Mine Bochnia, where the state is a 30 % owner of the venture and the sole owner of the salt mine itself), and the local level (if, for example, local governments own land or properties leased to private enterprises or contributed as "assets in kind" to public-private partnership ventures).

2. Slow progress in state assets privatisation leads to negative economic consequences and limits the possibilities of EU assistance. State ownership of assets precludes such economic entities from obtaining non-repayable financial assistance. Assistance of this kind is only available in the case of so-called soft projects, such as staff training, or in the case of daughter-companies established with the use of entirely private capital, which allows such companies to apply for financial assistance to purchase machinery.

3. A serious barrier to entrepreneurship is the question of employment, specifically employee remuneration and staff rotation. As mentioned before, the problem is caused by labour migration in search for better pay. To provide services of the specific type, the company needs qualified personnel trained in diverse skills (hotel staff, health workers, able to work underground). At the same time the staff must display high people skills, such as assertiveness, hospitality, friendliness, punctuality, reliability, etc.

It seems inevitable that after the company has achieved its profitability targets it will have to increase the wages to ensure staff retention and a high quality of work. The present case study has shown that entrepreneurs can perform innovative activities even in the conditions of turbulent business surroundings. The studied case shows that innovative entrepreneurs are able to define the rules of markets in which they operate, create new markets and new needs, be proactive, and anticipate the moves of their competitors. Actions of innovative entrepreneurs place them among the leaders – trail-blazers – of markets where they are present.

The Spas of Salt Mine Bochnia with its innovative product has created new needs. The product core conceptualisation is unlike any product based on similar attractions – salt mines – offered in the market. The rate of visitor growth in all targeted segments shows that the innovative concept upon which the product core is based has gained tourists' approval.

Conditions for entrepreneurial development fall into two categories, i.e. created by companies for themselves, and external, such as government policy (G. Gołembski, 2008, p. 23). In the present study we have placed a great emphasis on the surroundings of the innovative entrepreneur, pointing to factors both hampering and stimulating the development of entrepreneurship and innovativeness. In a young market economy such as Poland there are numerous examples of actions taken at different levels of authority that are either hampering of facilitating entrepreneurial attitudes. Without a doubt, the lawmakers and governments are responsible for laying down favourable conditions for entrepreneurial activities by giving access to land set aside for investments, construction and modernisation of technical infrastructure and utilities, or through incentives such as tax breaks. In the study we also point out that unfinished privatisation processes and the related political risk are liable to frustrate entrepreneurial ventures.

In conclusion, we may comment that entrepreneurial and innovative attitudes are most likely to thrive and bear fruit if companies looking for opportunities in the market can count on solid support from local governments.

References

Alejziak W. (1999), Turystyka w obliczu wyzwań XXI wieku, Albis, Kraków.

Briggs S. (2001), Successful Tourism Marketing, Kogan Page, London.

Drucker P. F. (1992), Innowacje i przedsiębiorczość, PWE.

Gadrey J., Gallouj F., Weinstein O. (1995), New modes of innovation. How services benefit industry, "International Journal of Service Industry Management", Vol. 6, No. 3.

Gołembski G. (2008), Methods of entrepreneurship research in the polish tourism sector, in: Entrepreneurship and quality in tourism in light of polish and international research, G. Gołembski (ed.), Wydawnictwo Akademii Ekonomicznej w Poznaniu, Poznań.

Gross Domestic Product by Voivodships (2003), GUS, Warszawa.

Mattsson J., Sundbo J., Fussing-Jenes Ch (2005), Innovation Systems in Tourism: The Roles of Attractors and Scene-Takers, "Industry and Innovation", Vol. 12, Iss. 3.

Niezgoda A., Zmyślony P. (2003), Popyt turystyczny, AE, Poznań.

Stevenson H.H., Jarillo J. C. (1990), A Paradigm of Entrepreneurship: Entrepreneurial Management, "Strategic Management Journal", Vol. 11.

Świtalski W., Innowacje i konkurencyjność (2005), Wydawnictwo Uniwersytetu Warszawskiego, Warszawa.

Tkaczyk T. T. (2000), Przedsiębiorczość a strategie konkurencji, Oficyna Wydawnicza Szkoły Głównej Handlowej, Warszawa.

Tourism alternatives cd (1995), V.L. Smith and W.R. Eadington John Willey & sons.

ALISON MORRISON AND PAUL LYNCH

The Case of Howard Wilkinson and the Ayrshire Food Network

1   Introduction

The Scottish Food and Drink Strategy devised by the key economic development bodies of Scottish Enterprise (SE) and Highlands and Island Enterprise (HIE) sets out its vision for the future as follows:

"Scottish food and Drink industry is **thriving internationally**, with an unrivalled reputation for high quality, natural products which are completely in tune with international consumer tastes. Industry and supporting organisations operate in a climate of trust and mutual respect, with **strong linkages across the cluster** – between farmers, fishermen, processors and customers. The whole industry is pulling in one direction, with a **culture of innovation**, and investment in people, processes and marketing. These changes **attract ambitious young people** into a vibrant industry".

Creating vision statements is the easy part. The tough task is to translate it into a grass root level reality, engaging the farmers, fishermen, processors and customers in a sustainable manner. "That's not so difficult", says Howard Wilkinson who is described as an influential, visionary, and collaborative community entrepreneur. He goes on to explain that: "if you view life in the form of the Olympic Games logo – a set of overlapping rings with soft edges, like pods letting you step from one to another – then you can achieve the vision". Nice analogy that on the face of it appears tinged with a form of romanticism. Not so. Evidence of the translation of the SE/HIE vision into a grass root initiative can be seen embodied in the Ayrshire Food Network (AFN), an innovative idea that is championed by Howard who currently participates in it as a member and Chairman. It grew out of a Culture and Heritage Project set up by the regional tourism forum that had a sub-focus on Food/Gastronomy. AFN is described as: an informal network involving artisan food producers and fine food providers who use the best of Scottish produce from Ayrshire. Its purpose is to promote the creation and production within Ayrshire of artisan food and drink, its usage and consumption by way of a network of businesses in Ayrshire and surrounding environs.

AFN is has thirty-five members, the majority of which are small- or micro-sized enterprises. The membership consists of restaurants, primary producers, coffee shops, specialist suppliers and shops, and hotels and bed and breakfast tourist accommodation. AFN could be described as an anti-response to globalisation believing in the need to preserve biodiversity, encourage food supply traceability and the reduction of food miles. It represents a geographic, business and tourism cluster that is concerned with sustainability across economic, social, environmental and tourism criteria. Cohesion and consolidation allows the coming together of food, culture and heritage – optimising the fact that Scotland's best-loved poet Robert Burns was born in Ayrshire, along with the beautiful natural environment, fertile farming and colourful historical legacy. AFN is supported by private enterprises and public sector agencies at regional, local, national and European levels. In addition, it networks with:

- A local Further Education college (Kilmarnock) that has had access to Objective 3 European Funding – SME Learning Networks;
- An associated international network that share similar network aims and configurations in Finland and Sweden (www.skargardssmak.com);
- The Ayrshire Farmers Market, a co-operative of primary producers, some of the membership of which is shared with AFN;
- Lobbyist organisations, such as the Slow Food Movement established in Italy in 1986 with 83,000 members internationally that promotes food and wine culture, and defends food and agricultural biodiversity worldwide; and
- Involvement in an associated international business partnership organised under the European Funded DART programme (www.interreg-dart.com) involving Cork, Republic of Ireland and Hunsruck, Germany and the South Ayrshire council, building on the opportunities afforded by the 14 Ryanair low cost airline routes working out of Prestwick Airport, and the associated 2.6 million passengers moving through the airport and adjacent areas.

Started in 2003, AFN is primarily a distribution and marketing network. There is a commitment among members to deliver a total quality customer/tourist experience as manifested through their small- and micro-enterprises, their products and traditions. This has been enhanced through customer service training for members and other training initiatives. Joint marketing activity takes the form of the production of a multi-lingual brochure that is distributed at Prestwick Airport and to 4,500 hotel bedrooms in Ayrshire. AFN participated and presented at the Slow Food's 2004 Terra Madre Conference in Turin that brought together 5,000 food producers from approximately 130 different countries. The presentation focused on sustainable tourism and the use of local food produce.

A sophisticated e-business portal has been established that facilitates an on-line community, encouraging and maximising business-to-business opportunities and promotion to consumers (www.inandaroundayrshire.com and www.ayrshirefarmersmarket.co.uk). The portal also promotes inter-supplier trading arrangements, and the appearance of links to other AFN members on individual member's web pages. With the assistance of Scottish Enterprise/Highlands and Islands Enterprise's Tourism Innovation Toolkit (www.scottish-enterprise.com), which contains a range of practical tips, techniques and tool to enable businesses to be more creative, more innovative and more successful, AFN developed the Ayrshire Experience Box. It is made up of a selection of food, information about Robert Burns, a music CD, maps and details of Ayrshire food producers and the Food Trail (Scottish Enterprise, 2005). At a regional level, this enhanced business activity provides an attraction and employment opportunities for the young to remain in the locality rather than to migrate to the cities.

Thus, returning to the SE/HEI vision for the future statement, it is evident that at a regional level AFN can demonstrate that it is thriving internationally. Within only a few years, it has established a presence and awareness with international travellers arriving through Prestwick Airport, in the regional tourist accommodation, on the international stage of the Slow Food conference in Turin, and working in tandem with other similar networks in Finland, Sweden, Italy, Republic of Ireland and Germany. It has established strong linkage across the cluster through a diverse but cohesive membership that somehow have "glued" together to enable the development and growth of a community of interest towards a sustainable, collective and common good for all stakeholders concerned. A culture of innovation appears to permeate the network drawing in the experience of members and the extended configuration of horizontal, vertical and diagonal networks. In turn, these innovatory and business performance optimising activities generate a greater industry cluster vibrancy that has improved potential to attract ambitious young people.

As the owner of a micro-business himself (Petrie Fine Foods that specialises in Vegetarian and Gluten-free produce which he runs in partnership with his wife Eileen), AFN's Chairman Howard Wilkinson concludes that: "you don't have to be big to do something rather special. It's about thinking collaboratively. On our own we're nothing. Working with other people we are rather special". This reinforces Howard's Olympic ring analogy where significant innovation and business performance achievement is secured for individual members and AFN collectively through the astute engineering of a composition of interlinked, overlapping, complementary networks of networks.

2 The Analysis

However, the foregoing has presented a surface level account of one example of tourism entrepreneurial innovation through networks. What it fails to do is to draw to the surface the relationships, dynamics and characteristics that are bubbling underneath – the aspects and architecture that scaffold the "public face" of AFN. Specifically it is does not identify the source and determinants of innovation, or the challenges relative to innovation and management that may have contributed to the network's success to date. These are now analysed within a framework that has been previously identified by Morrison, Lynch and Johns (2004) as relevant to international tourism network success and sustainability over their life cycle.

2.1 Objectives and Purpose

The objective is for members to work collectively to achieve the common purpose stated above, towards the leverage and mobilisation of economic, social and tourism assets and resources. It represents a local supply chain reflecting regional traditions, culture and heritage. There is a strong sense of commitment to doing this within an agenda that has sustainability as a high priority. This is achieved within a culture that promotes innovation and a community of learning through networks that is in tune with the politics of the day and hierarchy. Consequently, there is clarity as regards networking goals, geographic scope and remit, and the linking of aims to local, regional, national and international priorities enable the network to transcend issue that may deflect the driving purpose of the network.

2.2 Organisational Structure and Leadership

At the AFN level, the organisational structure is informal; it is not a legal entity, as this was the preferred model for government support agencies from which the network was seeking funding support. Thus, it can be described as a private/public network, driven by the private sector members in partnership. However, it should be thought of in terms of a circle within the "Olympic Games" logo to understand that a composite network of networks has been created, meshing and interconnecting in a manner that is complimentary. This reflects a more complex and multi-dimensional organisational structure, involving diagonal, horizontal and vertical creative linkages as appropriate to time and purpose. Furthermore, these arrangements evolve and have "soft edges", or certain fluidity. This recognises that human beings with ever changing priorities, life-stages and general circumstances populate networks. Within such a hybrid and informal structure, the network leader could be termed as a "pioneer", "champion" or "entrepreneur" – in Howard Wilkinson's words – a "social engineer", who plays a vital catalytic role. He brings his own world view that allows him to see: "twists, angles and connections allowing creative combinations of apparently dispirit entities to come together to benefit agents and agencies alike". This opens up new ways of working, innovation and business re-engineering. He has skills that have been finely tuned in the international corporate environment brought to bear in his voluntarily downshifted life. Hard skills are relative to leading edge information technology communication, business development and financial management. Soft skills include: patience, listening skills, and empathy to massage entities together and connect them; sound inter-personal skills that are both sensitive and directive to facilitate the buy in from stakeholders; and high political astuteness and alertness to optimise the potential of mutually beneficial outcomes. With respect to the last skill, Howard observed that: "I know how to 'press the right buttons' to move forward my business, the network's and the partners' agendas at the same time. This works on the basis of complimentarity at all levels".

2.3   Resourcing

The network is in the early stages of its life cycle and to date financial resourcing has been leveraged in pockets from various support agencies. On their own they represent relatively insignificant amounts, however, their collective critical mass has resulted in key advancements, such as, the development of the multi-lingual brochure and on-line business communities. To a large extent, the human resourcing has been "in kind" with voluntary contributions being drawn in from AFN members and through the extended "Olympic Games" network. This brings into play the concepts of network sustainability and life cycle. Howard Wilkinson believes that networks do have finite life cycles and unless they are continuously refreshed with new ideas and members they may lose their dynamism, innovatory capacity and become dysfunctional, at which point the most useful thing to do is to destroy them and move on. This opens thinking relative to the heterogeneity of networks where a goal of sustainability in some cases may be inappropriate, whereas a goal of short-term coupling to achieve short-term gains would be appropriate. That said, continuity of adequate financial, human and physical resources to satisfy the objectives and purpose of a network is critical to a network's success and sustainable generation of desired benefits.

2.4 Member Engagement

The Chairman of the network plays a key and essential role in member engagement, and this is particularly where his sound people skills and ability to empathise come into play. Members are united in an agreed common purpose, each bringing complimentary business and tourist offerings to the network, and are engaged in the decision-making process. Legitimisation of the network builds as tangible evidence of progress and gains are demonstrated, for example, an increase in turnover through inter-member trading. This impacts on the sustainability of credibility of the Chairman and the increased propensity of other players to want to be involved with the network. In addition, the clustered community nature of AFN within a micro-society plans an important part in its effective functioning. Member engagement represents a significant challenge relative to innovation, management and network sustainability. It is achieved through a comprehensive understanding, interlinking and management of a diverse set of member motivations including economic, social and psychological.

2.5 Benefits and Inter-Organisational Learning

Members can identify a causal relationship between membership and increased levels of trading. Fairly primitive distribution channels have been revolutionised through the likes of international marketing, promotion of the tourist food trail, embracing technological advances enabling on-line trading and the consolidation of products into easily purchasable packages. This has had a cascade effect within the region where it has impacted on tourist numbers, employment opportunities, and community involvement and spirit. AFN has advanced the ecological and authenticity cause relative to the traceability of produce, reduction in food miles that also ensures that economic benefits are retained within the regional system. However, a paradox arises in that the majority of members in AFN are happy to enjoy increased economic activity – but not so much that they will need to grow. Many are like Howard Wilkinson, they have made a conscious life-style choice that they want to keep their business small. For example, he describes himself in Maslow's hierarchy of needs terms as in a "self-actualisation" mode. This suggests a glass ceiling for AFN with respect to business development. Inter-organisational learning takes place mainly informally, although evidence of formal knowledge transfer from the AFN to like organisations in the Republic of Ireland, Finland, Sweden, Germany and Italy were noted. Furthermore, active and formal engagement with Kilmarnock College relative to SME learning provides further evidence of the organisational configuration providing the architecture for a learning community. Thus, AFN represents an example of a hub organisation and network members connected in a supportive infrastructure of formal and informal mechanisms. This facilitates inter-organisational learning and exchange that has the potential to translate into qualitative and/or qualitative benefits.

References

Augustyn, M., Knowles, t. (2000), Performance of tourism partnerships: a focus on York, in: Tourism Management, Vol. 21, pp. 341–51.

Halme, M. (2001), Learning for sustainable development in tourism networks, in: Business Strategy and the Environment, Vol. 10, pp. 100–14.

Lynch, P. (2000), Networking in the homestay sector, in: The Services Industries Journal, Vol. 20, No. 3, pp. 95–116.

Morrison, A. (1998), Small firm co-operative marketing in a peripheral tourism region, in: International Journal of Contemporary Hospitality Management, Vol. 10, No. 5, pp. 191–197.

Morrison, A., Lynch, P., Johns, N. (2004), International Tourism Networks, in: International Journal of Contemporary Hospitality Management, Vol. 16, No. 3, pp. 198–204.

Rogerson, C. (2003), Tourism and local economic development: the case of the highlands meander, in: Development Southern Africa, Vol. 19, pp. 143–67.

Scottish Enterprise (2005), Tourism Innovation in Action, No. 3, Scottish Enterprise, Glasgow.

Telfer, D. (2001), Strategic alliances along the Niagara wine route, in: Tourism Management, Vol. 22, pp. 21–30.

Acknowledgement:

Thanks is extended to Howard Wilkinson of Petrie Fine Foods, West Langton Farm, Dunlop, Ayrshire, Scotland (www.realproduce.co.uk) for the time he invested with the authors in interview, provision of extensive secondary support information, and verification of the case study content as it went through its development.

BARTOLOMÉ DEYÁ TORTELLA AND MARÍA RAZUMOVA

Innovation and Sustainability in a Mass Tourism Destination – The Green Card in the Balearic Islands

1   Tourism, Innovation and Sustainability: the Case of the Balearic Islands

Today tourism is one of the main driving forces of economic growth in Spain, especially for the Balearic Islands. According to UNWTO, in 2005, Spain was second in the world in terms of international tourist arrivals (55.6 million people) and international tourism receipts (47.9 billion USD), up 6 % and 5.8 % respectively from the 2004 figures (Economic Research Center, 2005; World Tourism Organization, 2006). Within Spain, the Balearic Islands (Mallorca, Menorca, Ibiza and Formentera) were second only to the Catalonia region receiving 9.6 million tourists and EUR 8.52 billion in tourism receipts (Economic Research Center, 2005). The service sector represents around 80 % of the GDP of the Islands, with the share related directly to tourism about 53.3 %. Additionally, some recent estimates indicate that approximately 84.4 % of total Balearic GDP is directly or indirectly related to tourism activities. These data show that tourism is extremely important for the Balearic economy and for its society, bringing wealth, business and a high standard of living to the islands.

The next important objective for the region is to achieve sustainable tourism development. The current tourism model has resulted in serious environmental problems. For example, congestion is a major issue. In 2005, the number of international tourists per resident was 9.8, and the number per square meter of territory and per meter of coastline was 1.9 and 6.7 respectively. These indicators of congestion are even more worrying if one takes into account the seasonal character of tourist arrivals to the Balearic Islands. Most tourists arrive in the summer months (from June to September), looking for the traditional sun and sand type of vacation. The direct consequences are traffic jams, crowded beaches, water supply problems and increased pressure on the waste and sewage treatment facilities. Therefore it becomes apparent that the Balearic Islands need a new approach which will guarantee long-term sustainable development.

The concept of Sustainable Development was coined at the Earth Summit, celebrated in Rio de Janeiro in 1992. This summit established Sustainable Development as the greatest challenge to be met by society during the new century. Sustainable development is what makes it possible to satisfy the needs of present generations without jeopardising the capacity of future generations. The three dimensions of the concept (economic, social and environmental) are closely linked to the taking of responsibility by the present generation. Sustainable development takes into account the relationship between the environment, and the social and economic spheres. It attempts to harmonise human activity, while respecting nature and culture, and ensuring the well-being of society. The Rio de Janeiro summit achieved a series of compromises by the states, and through initiatives and directives it aimed to reorient public administration to gear policies and actions towards the promotion of natural spaces, non-contaminating energies, recycling, and in a special way, promoting the awareness of sustainability to the general population and to companies.

Sustainability is becoming an increasingly important concept for the tourism sector as has been pointed out in many international meetings and seminars (e.g. Quebec Declaration on Ecotourism, World Summit on Sustainable Development – Plan of Implementation). In the last Seminar on Policies, Strategies and Tools for Sustainable Tourism Development organised by the UNWTO Commission for Europe in Almati (Kazakhstan, April 2006), several important conclusions were reached. During this seminar the importance of developing "… policies and planning in order to raise the sustainability of tourism and increase the contribution of tourism to the overall sustainable development of societies" was emphasized (Conclusions of the first session on Tourism and Sustainability, page 1). The current high growth rate in European tourism implies there is increasing pressure on the natural and cultural resources of the tourism destinations. One of the final suggestions of the seminar, in line with recent UNWTO recommendations to public institutions, is the need to develop initiatives which will allow economic growth while maintaining the cultural and environmental goals of the region.

In this context, the innovative initiative chosen to be discussed here is the Green Card developed in June 2005 by the Foundation for Sustainable Development in the Balearic Islands. This paper demonstrates that this is a good example of an initiative developed by a public institution, aimed at creating a long-term sustainable development model in the tourism sector. The European Parliament in 2005 hailed the Green Card as a pioneering and exemplary initiative to help raise funds for the protection and improvement of the environment, and encouraged other European regions to take steps in the same direction.

2 The Foundation for Sustainable Development in the Balearic Islands: Recognition of the Sustainability Problems of the Balearic Mass Tourism Destination

In the last decade there has been growing recognition of the need to achieve long-term sustainable economic development all over the world. Public institutions are being forced to develop initiatives which will reconcile economic growth with the environmental and cultural resources of the society.

The Balearic Islands have not kept aloof from this world trend. The limited resources of the islands (especially significant in terms of land and space), and the general problems related to tourism saturation directly attributable to the current tourism model, led the Balearic society to realise the necessity of developing a new model of tourism, based on tourism development compatible with specific environmental and cultural aspects of the Islands.

To meet these demands, in July 2004, the Balearic Islands Government created the Foundation for Sustainable Development in the Balearic Islands (FSDBI). To encourage private businesses to take an active part in this initiative (which was considered crucial for the success of the project) the Foundation's Board of Trustees was composed of representatives of the Balearic Islands Government and of the most important Spanish financial entities (Banco de Santander, Banco Bilbao Vizcaya Argentaria, Banca March, Caja de Ahorros del Mediterraneo, Sa Nostra Caja de Baleares). The priority of the FSDBI is to promote initiatives that can help the Balearic Islands to become a sustainable tourist destination in the mid-term. Therefore, its main objectives can be summarized as follows:

- Make residents and tourists aware of the environmental, heritage and cultural values of the Islands, and the importance of their preservation and protection.
- Teach and inform both residents and visitors about the balance between human activity and the environment, the necessity for sustainable development, and the recognition of the importance of environmental resources.
- Fund raise in order to financially support projects to be held in natural and cultural settings, and initiatives which strive for sustainability. These funds are to be obtained from many sources, like the Green Card

fees, merchandising, private financing, and European projects related to sustainable development. During 2006 the Foundation raised EUR 2.4 million.

• Promote the Balearic Islands as a sustainable tourism destination.

Each financial year the Foundation's Board of Trustees selects the projects to be financed and priority is always given to projects which best respond to the principal aim of the Foundation: the rehabilitation and improvement of the important natural and cultural sites of the Islands. One of the completed projects is the rehabilitation of the emblematic Sant Nicolau Castle in Menorca which was constructed in 1575 and receives approximately 10.000 visitors per year. Another significant example is the development of the National Park of S'Albufera on Mallorca which receives approximately 65.000 visitors per year. The development improved access to the park and various routes within it, especially for visitors with limited mobility. Other minor projects include measures that increase the awareness of residents and visitors to the Islands' environmental and cultural heritage, a free bicycle service in the national parks and other sites of special interest, green workshops for adults and children, and seminars on sustainable development for local businesses.

One of the most important projects of the Foundation is the Green Card (Tarjeta Verde). The Green Card is a novel and efficient way to obtain resources to finance initiatives for the preservation and protection of sensitive natural and cultural sites, and at the same time make residents and visitors aware of the importance of sustainable tourism.

3   The Green Card

The Green Card was one of the first initiatives undertaken by the FSDBI to raise funds and has been one of its most prominent projects. The Green Card represents an innovative move within the tourism sector. The purchase of the Card is voluntary and the Card holder is actively contributing towards the finance of projects dedicated to the conservation and improvement of natural and cultural assets of the tourist destination.

3.1   How does the Green Card work?

The Green Card was launched in May of 2005. The selling price is EUR 10, and the validity period is 15 days. The Green Card has two main objectives. Firstly, it aims to raise funds to finance projects to protect and improve the Balearic Islands' cultural and natural heritage. (In the first year 1 euro from every card sold was donated to help the victims of the tsunami in Asia.) Secondly, it is a means to increase visitors' awareness of the importance of sustainable tourism and to encourage them to support its development in the Balearic Islands. The Green Card enables its holder to obtain discounts in more than 1.400 establishments, principally national parks, museums and cultural centres, but also shops and restaurants, travel and sport packages, leisure services, etc. It also offers discounts for public transport, renting of bicycles, parking, etc. Due to the voluntary nature of the Green Card, one of the main issues during the launch was how to encourage visitors to buy one. Today the Green Card may be bought at hotel receptions, on flights to the Balearic Islands, at tour operators and travel agents, at post offices, at the entities participating in the project, and in many other places. Currently, the Card may be purchased in approximately 1.800 establishments, on the Foundation's web site and by phoning the Green Card's call-center.

The Card buyer receives a package in Spanish, English or German, consisting of the Card, a welcome letter, an information leaflet, and a selection of guides and maps of the area were the tourist is located, to help him/her to make the most of what the Green Card has to offer. It also contains a magazine which provides the buyer with information about the establishments where the Card can be used, and of the corresponding discounts. At the same time, it presents the principal objectives of the Card, and the underlying philosophy and the main actions of the FSDBI. The magazine also includes detailed information about the projects financed by the Green Card. The final aim is to make the buyer an active co-participant in the project, and to make him/her conscious of the importance of sustainable tourism to the Balearic Islands.

The Green Card has a 24 hour call-centre where the Card buyer can obtain information about the use of the card, public transport and centres affiliated with the Green Card, and to resolve any doubt related to it.

Figure 1: The Green Card

3.2   Initial Commercialisation Strategy for the Green Card

The commercialisation strategy followed during the first year of the Card had several focuses. The first was the introduction of the Green Card onto the market. Given the novelty and voluntary character of the initiative it was crucial that the Card's potential buyer got to know "a priori" the main objectives of the project. In order to meet this aim a large marketing campaign was conducted, including presentations at the most important world tourism fairs (ITB-Berlin, World Travel Market-London, Reisepavillon, Fitur-Madrid), and to the most important tour operators and travel agents all over Europe.

The marketing campaign was also conducted with a number of important airlines, where commercials and video advertisements were placed. Additionally, marketing activities were developed at the destination. They took place in the main airports of the three islands, and in the most important tourist centres. Basically, the principal objectives of the campaign were to inform visitors about the Green Card, the benefits it can give, and of its underlying philosophy.

Simultaneously, it was necessary to take measures to develop and stimulate the supply side. One of the main tasks was to enrol a significant number of businesses into the project where the Card could be bought and used. The distribution strategy was focused mainly on hotels, and now approximately 35 % of the total number of Cards is sold through this distribution channel. Given the voluntary nature of the Card's acquisition, a key issue for the project's success was to educate and motivate potential distributors about the benefits of being involved. Only in this way could the spirit of the project be transmitted to potential Card buyers. The employees working at the distribution points were trained by the Green Card commercial team. The economic incentive for the distributor was set at EUR 2 from each Card sold.

The initial strategy for choosing establishments where the Card holder could obtain discounts was to include national parks and cultural centres (museums, emblematic buildings, etc.). This fulfilled one of the main objectives of the Green Card, that is, to make visitors familiar with the natural and cultural heritage of the Islands. Once these initial places were included, in order to make the Card more attractive to the visitor, participation in the Green Card project was opened up to other types of entities: restaurants, car hire establishments, shops, leisure services, etc.

Participation in the Project is absolutely free for the entity and the decision on the discount provided to the Card holder is determined by the entity's management. The discounts vary from 100 % in the case of bicycle rent, 50 % in museums, cultural and natural centres, and up to 10 % in other types of businesses. The benefits that the entity enjoys in exchange for participation in the project are the promotion and advertisement provided by the information package given with the Green Card. In this way, for example, entities which due to their size cannot afford marketing or promotional activities are able to reach an important market segment of visitors. The number of participants increased from 74 in May 2005 (when the project started) to 1.400 in December 2006. An interesting indicator of the good acceptance of the project among the participating entities is that, to date, no entity has ceased its participation in the project.

3.3 Perspectives for the Future

The results of the first year after launching the Card (period May of 2005 – May of 2006) are as follows: A total of 307.554 Green Cards was sold through the network of 1.800 points of distribution, and 1.400 entities decided to participate in the project by offering discounts. The sales of the Green Card generated EUR 2.46 million to finance the Foundation projects. Based on these results the foundation set the following two groups of objectives for the next period.

From the demand side of the project, the next task is to increase both the Green Card sales and its utilization by buyers. To achieve this, future marketing campaigns will be conducted in the countries of origin of visitors (participation in most important tourism fairs, collaboration with airlines, tour operators, travel agents, etc.), as well as in the destination (information points at hotel receptions, magazines in hotel rooms, information in the shuttle buses, merchandising and so on). Another option investigated by the Foundation is the creation of a one-day Green Card for the short-stay tourists who visit the islands during cruise tours or on weekends.

On the supply side, the next focus is on the development of loyalty, education, new incentives, and on the follow-up of the Card supply-side agents. To achieve these objectives, first of all, special attention is being given to the design of a web-site which will be exclusively for the card sellers, distributors and participating businesses. This web site will enable them to resolve doubts regarding the Card, and to receive updated information about it. Additionally, it is planned to use the web site for online in-company training. To give an additional incentive for the distribution and utilization of the Card, the Foundation is studying the possibility of launching a Fidelity Program for the Card distributors and participating businesses. In order to keep on improving the Card's performance and its utilisation, it is planned to install special software at the Card's distributing entities and in the establishments providing discounts. This software will allow a database to be generated encompassing information about the Card buyers, such as age, nationality, family profile, type of vacations, and where the card was used, etc. The database will be useful for planning new marketing campaigns, and for improving card design and distribution.

4 Conclusions

The Balearic Islands are a good example of how the tourism sector can become a driving force for economic and social progress in a whole region. At the same time, it is also a good example of how such growth may have serious problems on long term sustainability, particularly when tourism is based on models such as mass sun and sand tourism.

To meet the need for sustainable development, the Foundation for Sustainable Development in the Balearic Islands created an innovative instrument analyzed in this work – the Green Card. This voluntary and participative initiative was designed to meet the double objectives of generating funds to finance cultural and environmental projects of the Foundation and increase the awareness of the importance of the cultural and natural heritage of the Balearic Islands. During its first year the Green Card generated EUR 2.46 million for the Foundation's projects. The example of the Green Card shows that voluntary initiatives have significant potential for the development of a sustainable tourism model. Long term sustainability is becoming the main concern of many tourism destinations, encouraging them to adopt measures that can mitigate any negative cultural and environmental impacts of tourism. In this sense the innovative initiative of FSDBI, the Green Card, may be of interest to destinations looking for a way to achieve sustainable tourism development.

References

Economic Research Center, (2005), Informe Economic I Social, 2005. Universitat Illes Balears – Sa Nostra.

World Tourism Organization, (2006), Tourism Market Trends, 2006 Edition: Europe. World Tourism Organization.

WERNER BERNET AND PETER KELLER

Swiss Travel Bank (REKA) – Entrepreneurship and Innovation in a Non-Profit Organisation (NPOs)

1 Areas of Inquiry

Innovation is the motor of growth in a market economy. Innovations increase prosperity and improve the quality of life. They are usually the work of creative entrepreneurs who are not afraid of risks, and who in an effort to beat the competition come up with new products and processes that help penetrate new business areas. These entrepreneurs are above all motivated by a desire to find profitable business opportunities.

The Swiss Travel Bank (REKA) is one of our most innovative and successful tourism enterprises. Thanks to far-reaching innovations it created new additional value. During the past two decades of shrinking demand for Swiss tourism products and services, the Travel Bank nonetheless managed to double growth in core areas.

This amazing success raises a series of questions, since it is due neither to independent entrepreneurial innovators nor to a profit motive. This social tourism institution indeed relies on support from a great many quarters. It offers services in the public interest and is a non-profit organisation.

2 Nature of the Institution
2.1 Vision of Social Tourism

The Swiss Travel Bank (REKA) is the nation's leading institution in the area of social tourism. Its offer of traveller's cheques at reduced rates encourages putting aside money for holidays and thus the consumption of tourism services by a broader range of social classes. The REKA has in particular developed a wide range of holiday accommodation solutions for families with young children. It ranks as Switzerland's second most important supplier in the parahotel sector.

167

The revenue from capital employed from the growing volume of cheques is used to reduce the cost of the cheques. The proceeds are also used to finance a rapid depreciation of holiday installations, which in turn enables the Travel Bank to keep prices at the same level even during school holidays in the peak season. It also offers free holidays to families that are economically and socially disadvantaged. The Travel Bank is thus a commercial operation, which uses its profits to create "social value". Even in such a prosperous land as Switzerland there are people who are economically and socially disadvantaged.

2.2 Impressive Performance

The REKA offers two basic products. It sells traveller's cheques as a method of payment. And it provides holiday accommodation intended for families. These two core activities have enjoyed steady growth since the Swiss Travel Bank's foundation. In 2005 the REKA sold traveller's cheques worth a total of around SFR 542 million. These cheques were issued to customers at a discount of around SFR 80 million or 15.9 per cent (Figure 1).

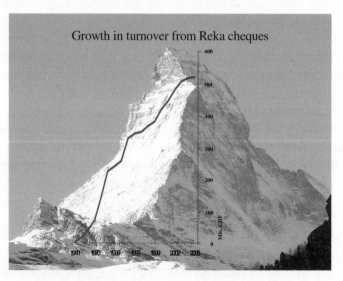

Figure 1: Growth in turnover from REKA cheques

The REKA cooperative society rented 494 of its own holiday homes and 771 properties belonging to third parties during the same year of 2005 in Switzerland. It also sold 229 "holidays on the farm". And it rented out 1,300 holiday homes abroad. This added up to around 1.3 million overnights and rental turnover of SFR 36 million.

3 Institutional Structures
3.1 Social Partnership: the Key to Success

The REKA is a public service cooperative society. Its foundation was assisted by a modest contribution from the Confederation as well as from employers and employees organisations. In 1936 employers in the Swiss machinery and metalworking industry and the trade unions signed a peace agreement. This obliged the two sides to settle labour disputes through negotiations rather than through strikes and lock-outs. Agreement was also reached on social benefits such as paid holidays, an arrangement that provided the basis for the spread of popular tourism in Switzerland, as in most of the industrial nations of the West.

The agreement of 1936 was the beginning of the fundamental Swiss social partnership that is still valid today, and which through the creation of the REKA was extended into the field of tourism. By reducing the price of the REKA traveller's cheques employers encourage travel. Reduced price traveller's cheques are still offered today as additional worker benefits and are tax-free.

3.2 Environment Conducive to Innovation

After the foundation of the Swiss Travel Bank the social partners have been careful to adopt a consistent market orientation. It was decided not to make use of state subsidies, for example in the form of any further reduction in the price of traveller's cheques.

Since the foundation of REKA efforts have been made to follow a clear strategy. The objectives are regularly reviewed with various in-house experts and client groups, evaluated in a transparent way and adopted on the basis of a consensus.

Part of the revenue from capital employed from unredeemed cheques is earmarked for research and development (R&D). The REKA is one of the few companies in the area of "incoming" tourism that have adopted innovation as a matter of routine.

The supervisory bodies responsible for the strategy of the Swiss Travel Bank are constantly in search of ways to strengthen the Bank's position while ensuring continuity in the management approach. The longevity of the management team is in fact high. Since its founding nearly 70 years ago the Swiss Travel Bank has had only four Directors.

4 Main Strategic Markers
4.1 Development of New Market Potential

The introduction of paid holidays was one of the major social innovations of the industrial society. Even so the budget of a worker's family with several children was often too small to pay for any kind of travel. And the tourism products on offer at the time were very limited. Without a special effort to put money aside, and accommodation suitable for families, travel was not an option for most workers.

The REKA took advantage of the rapid growth in the additional value in innovative ways. The creation of cheques helped solve the problem of saving for holidays and paying for the consumption of tourism products. The rental of accommodation suitable for family holidays was the final piece in the jigsaw puzzle. The Swiss Travel Bank succeeded in focusing clearly on the family segment of the market and in this way made a substantial contribution to the popularisation of tourism in Switzerland. Until the 1990s the Travel Bank's product range was limited to holiday accommodation in Switzerland. The purchase of the holiday village "Golfo del Sole" on the coast of Tuscany was the first in its catalogue of holiday home rentals abroad. Internationalisation of its products and services resulted in diversification at the parahotel level. Today in addition to holiday homes the range of products includes mobile homes and other types of accommodation.

4.2 Strategic Partnerships

The penetration of the Swiss travel market by the traveller's cheques of the Swiss Travel Bank required absolutely careful and consistent management of cooperation in both of the Bank's main product areas. The Bank persuaded an ever growing number of employers to offer traveller's cheques as fringe benefits. It also succeeded in convincing major distributors to offer the cheques to their clients at a discount. Furthermore systematic efforts were made to recruit companies willing to accept the cheques and pay a commission. The strategic partners, who today issue the cheques at a discount, in particular the chemical industry or the Coop retail outlet, are of the utmost importance for REKA. They have a determining influence on the size of the market for traveller's cheques. Equally important is cooperation with the companies that take the cheques. Particularly vital in this context are the public transport authorities. The economic success of the Swiss Travel Bank depends essentially on this cooperation based on long term relations secured on a contractual and institutional basis, in accordance with the "win-win" business principle.

Internationalisation of the holiday accommodation market as a core area of REKA activities led to new strategic partnerships including the Bank's French opposite number "VillageVacancesFamilles", and the Dutch company "SelectCamp".

5 Innovation as the Bedrock of Steady Growth
5.1 Travellers' Cheques as a Method of Payment in Tourism

The economic success of the REKA is based on the introduction of traveller's cheques as a method of payment. Their sale at a discounted price provided the necessary incentive to buy them. And since the cheque is not cashed until a later stage with the purchase of products and services, the effect is to encourage holiday savings. Traveller's cheques are issued by such Swiss employers as the Novartis chemical company, the Post Office (65.8 per cent) and the trade unions (5.7 per cent), as well as by Coop retail outlets (25.6 per cent) and the Manor department store chain (2.0 per cent).

Some 7,000 tourism enterprises are ready to accept traveller's cheques as a method of payment in Switzerland. They are prepared to pay the Swiss Travel Bank a commission of 3–4 per cent. Roughly half of the traveller cheques in 2005 went to public transport companies and in particular Swiss Federal Railways and Swiss Airlines, while 20 per cent were paid to petrol stations, about 12 per cent to cable car operators, 7.4 per cent to the hotel and catering sector and approximately 5.6 per cent to travel agents. A brief description of the REKA cheque cycle shows the cleverness of this Swiss innovation in social tourism, which to date no other country has succeeded in imitating fully. Taking advantage of the income it gets from the commission the REKA reduces the cost of the cheque by 1.5 per cent. Those who issue the cheques to the public discount them by an average of 16 per cent, while most employers reduce the price by 20 per cent. Thus a cheque with a face value of SFR 100 is sold to the consumer for just SFR 80. The consumer spends the full amount at face value on tourism products and services (Figure 2).

REKA cheques as innovation

Figure 2: REKA cheque as innovation

5.2 Creative Imitation in the Parahotel Sector

The Swiss Travel Bank began at an early stage renting family holiday accommodation for third parties, an area in which it is still active today. Inspired by its experiences with holiday rentals REKA began to invest in holiday villages in 1960. The 600 or so holiday homes it offers in 21 villages are among the most sought after products today.

REKA holiday villages are not simply an attempt to copy the social tourism innovations of others, the most obvious example being the "Club Méditerannée". The holiday villages operated by REKA are all adapted specifically to Swiss requirements. In particular they offer the high level of comfort and convenience which the Swiss expect. Each village has its own indoor swimming pool together with other sporting facilities. A special effort is made to provide entertainment for children, notably through a programme run by professionals known as "Rekalino".

The REKA Family Holidays Fund ensures a comparatively speedy depreciation of the infrastructure, so that unlike its competitors the Travel Bank is able to offer prices that are attractive to families even during school holidays in the peak season.

6 Further Development of Core Products

6.1 IT supported Value Card: REKA Check Card

Currently the company is introducing a remarkable innovation in the market for traveller's cheques. The product range, which continues to include traditional paper traveller's cheques, is to be completed by a Value Card. This will enable the REKA cheque user to make paperless transactions. As well as providing additional customer convenience the "REKA-cheque-Card" helps to rationalise the travellers cheque cycle and reduce the number of cash-like cheques in circulation.

The "REKA Check Card" has been developed in collaboration with the Swiss Post Office, which with "Post Finance" as bank services who produces the "Postcard". The most commonly found and used Value Card in Switzerland. Thanks to this collaborative effort the cost of the development and technology was reduced to around SFR 1 million.

6.2 Theme Villages: a New Kind of Investment and Symbiosis between Agriculture and Tourism

A theme village is currently being developed in an agricultural area in the alpine foothills below Säntis (Urnäsch AI) as a pilot project. The idea is to take advantage of synergies between agriculture and tourism. Families with children will be able to count on all the comfort of a Swiss holiday village, and will at the same time have a unique opportunity to learn about farming as a way of life with its own cultural richness. The local farming community is 100 per cent behind the project.

Given the increasing signs of saturation in the Swiss holiday accommodation market the Swiss Travel Bank is doing its best to reduce investment risks. It is not in fact involved in the theme village as an investor. The necessary capital was raised through tourism policy and regional policy instruments, at the federal and cantonal levels (promotion of innovation and cooperation in tourism, assistance with investment in remote mountainous areas) and with the support of others through the local authorities. REKA's involvement is limited to the operation of the new village, starting in 2008, while guaranteeing rentals over the long term.

7   Implications for the Economy
7.1   Positive Externalities

The Swiss Travel Bank is a "brand" with a high recognition value among the Swiss population and a very good reputation. Throughout its life it has contributed much to the achievement of social policy objectives through the promotion of holidays for the family. Thanks to REKA people from all social classes are able to take holidays in Switzerland and abroad. REKA has also contributed to the success of regional policy. Most of its holiday villages have been developed outside the main tourism centres. Despite this it has managed to achieve high rates of occupancy even in peripheral areas, and in this way to create employment and a source of income to economically depressed areas. Most REKA holiday villages have an occupancy rate of 300 days or more in a year.

7.2   Swiss Parahotel Initiative

Switzerland has an extensive and highly diversified range of holiday accommodation. Not enough use is made of this trump card of Swiss tourism. The average annual occupancy rate of holiday accommodation is below 20 per cent. Too little is invested in the renewal of installations and equipment.

REKA has provided the leadership for a new Swiss initiative in the parahotel segment, an initiative which has the support of the Innovation Programme of the State Secretariat for Economic Affairs (seco). An "electronic marketplace" has been created in collaboration with Switzerland Tourism (NTO). Furthermore, individual holiday homes in tourism centres are to be pooled in a "cluster" arrangement. The "holiday homes in Switzerland" e-market offers a bird's eye view of all available rentals in this field. The website, which is accessible to the general public, includes 15,000 holiday homes listed by the Swiss Tourism Industries Association, all vetted for quality. Only properties that are actually available appear on the screen, and these can be booked in a decentralised way from individuals concerned, without the payment of a commission. The website is open to all, the only requirement being that the property must be currently available for rental. This e-market is a Swiss world première (Figure 3).

Creation of an e-marketplace „Holiday homes of
Switzerland"

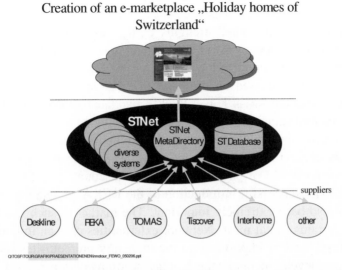

Figure 3: Creation of an e-marketplace "Holidays homes of Switzerland"

Moreover holiday accommodation that until now has been offered on the
market by local tourism organisations or private individuals will now be subject to quality control and rented in a professional manner through the creation of "holiday accommodation clusters" in tourism centres. These are to be
run by "Cluster Managers", whose job will be to ensure that basic services
are provided.

8   Conclusions
The growth of popular tourism in the industrialised world found the Swiss
Travel Bank poised and ready to take advantage of the additional value with
innovative products, and it managed to carve out a share of the market. It
succeeded in building strong networks and becoming one of Switzerland's
leading tourism enterprises. REKA is indeed a public service cooperative,
whose objectives can be described as "meta-economic". Despite the hetero-
geneous nature of the organisations behind it the Swiss Travel Bank has consistently been managed by men who have known how to develop a winning
strategy based on modern techniques. It is possible to distribute only what
has been earned in accordance with market economy criteria.

Unlike most other companies in the Swiss "incoming" business sector
REKA sees innovation as a production factor. Some of its profits are set aside
to finance a proactive investment policy for the innovative development and

marketing of its core products. This routine use of innovation has been a key success factor for REKA. Management of cooperation and the formation of strategic alliances are other strengths of the organisation. The success of REKA traveller's cheques is to a great extent due to the institutionalisation of successful efforts at cooperation in core product areas. Its partnerships have above all been concluded on the basis of "win-win" situations. The public service nature of the Swiss Travel Bank's mandate has also played a role.

The inherent social tourism orientation and the nature of the Swiss Travel Bank's core business will continue to determine its future course. A key factor in this context will be the continuing acceptance of REKA traveller's cheques as a method of payment. The price discount must therefore remain attractive. The successful introduction of the REKA cheque Card as a Value Card has also been extremely important. The market in such instruments requires a certain critical mass. Network externalities play an important role in this context. Next in importance to the monetary prerequisites for economic success are developments in the holiday accommodation market. Given the existing saturation and the expected downsizing of the "families with children" market segment in Switzerland, the internationalisation of supply and demand in this area will be a determining factor for success in the long term. In the same way as the integrated hotel chains the Swiss Travel Bank will have to ask itself whether its future lies in the area of real estate or more in the area of management contracts.

References

Bernet, W., Sozialtourismus: das Beispiel der REKA, Universität Bern, Februar 2006.

WILLIAM GARTNER

Carlson Destination Marketing Services

1 Introduction

Mission Statement of Carlson Destination Marketing Services is to help build mutually beneficial relationships between destination organizations and their channels. Building Partnerships: Building significant tourism relationships is our core strength. It is the springboard to client's long-term success.

Carlson Destination Marketing Services, based in Minneapolis, MN, delivers a wide range of marketing services to client destinations around the world. CDMS assists destination organizations in marketing themselves more effectively to the American and international traveler. Through strategic marketing, public relations and consulting services, CDMS has provided some of the most successful and cost-effective marketing strategies to destinations worldwide.

CDMS has all the advantages and benefits of being part of a global leader. We are able to leverage the vast resources of Carlson on behalf of our clients. Yet CDMS also offers the flexibility, speed and creativity associated with a small, entrepreneurial agency.

CDMS is part of a larger network of travel related businesses under the name of Carlson Leisure Group. Carlson, the parent company to CDMS, was founded in 1938. Carlson is a global leader in providing superior hospitality, travel and marketing services and solutions to corporate and consumer clients. Brands include, Radisson Hotels, Radisson Seven Seas Cruises, Country Inn and Suites, Regent International Hotels, Park Inn, Park Plaza, T.G.I. Fridays, Pick Up Stix, Provisions, Carlson Marketing Group, Carlson Wagonlit Travel, Cruise Holidays, Results Travel and Carlson Destination Marketing Services.

Some of Carlson's global resources that can benefit destinations include presence in over 140 countries, state-of-the-art call centers, fulfillment services, in-house creative services and strong relationships with major travel-industry suppliers.

CDMS researches its client's needs, their markets and their competitors markets thoroughly to first fully understand the current situation. In doing so, we pinpoint the destination's most fruitful target audiences and the best target medium by which to reach them. With the information we glean from this research, we then put together a strategically powerful and extremely targeted strategy for the organization.

CDMS will work with you to define your current market segments to build, maintain and enhance a targeted relationship marketing strategy while also maximizing your time and financial resources.

CDMS firmly believes that relationships are at the heart of every successful destination marketing program. CDMS' relationships are based on years of establishing strong working contacts in the travel industry. Because our company is part of one of the largest hospitality and marketing organizations in the world, we already have established relationships with many major players in the tourism distribution channel. In addition, our active role in the industry gives us a unique understanding of each group.

THE RELATIONSHIP PYRAMID

The Destination Relationship Model demonstrates how the different categorical groups involved in increasing tourism interact and depend on each other. The groups consist of: the destination organization, local stakeholders, media/travel agents/travel brokers, suppliers/partners and the consumer. To successfully market and maintain a destination, destination organizations need strong relationships with each group in the destination relationship model.

THE DESTINATION RELATIONSHIP MODEL

2   The Industry

CDMS is a full-service destination marketing service agency that provides marketing, public relations, representation, research and management solutions to destinations around the world. Unlike most marketing agencies, we work exclusively in the travel and tourism industry. Our knowledgeable staff offers expert advice gained from years of experience working in the travel and tourism industry.

3   Relationships

With the changing and fluid nature of the travel distribution channels, it is even more critical today that programs and services are built on strong relationships between destination organizations and their stakeholders, suppliers/partners, agents and consumers.

4   Resources

CDMS has all the advantages and benefits of being part of a global leader. We are able to leverage the vast resources of Carlson Companies on behalf of our clients. Yet CDMS also offers the flexibility, speed and creativity associated with a small, entrepreneurial agency.

5   Results

CDMS strives to deliver results for our clients. We know that effective destination marketing involves more than solid strategic planning and successful implementation. We start by working with the client to set goals. Then we create marketing and public relations plans with built-in measurement tools to benchmark results. CDMS supports its marketing and public relations efforts with useful pre- and post-implementation research to help you make informed decisions.

6   Clients
CDMS has built relationships for destination organizations with the Carlson Companies travel brands, Preferred Destination:
- Aruba Tourism Authority
- Bahamas Tourist Office
- Bermuda Department of Tourism
- Black Hills, Badlands and Lakes Association
- Canadian Tourism Commission
- Hong Kong Tourism Board
- Hawaii Visitors and Convention Bureau
- Israel Ministry of Tourism
- Japan National Tourist Organization
- Kenya Tourist Board
- Las Vegas Convention & Visitors Authority
- Lisbon Tourism Bureau
- Louisiana Office of Tourism
- Singapore Tourism Board
- Vail Resorts

7   Trade Partnership Relationships
- Alaska Travel Industry Association
- Anchorage Convention & Visitors Bureau
- Belgium Tourist Office
- Bloomington, Minnesota Convention & Visitors Bureau
- Croatian National Tourist Office
- Curacao Tourist Board
- French Government Tourist Office
- German National Tourist Office
- Greater Houston Convention & Visitor Bureau
- Greater Miami Convention & Visitors Bureau
- Jamaica Tourist Board
- Kissimmee Convention and Visitors Bureau
- Korea National Tourism Organization
- Lake Tahoe Visitors Authority

- Lee County Visitors & Convention Bureau
- Marianas Visitors Authority
- Monaco Government Tourist Office
- North Dakota Tourism Division
- Niue Island Tourism
- Orlando / Orange County Convention & Visitors Bureau, Inc.
- Palm Beach County Convention & Visitors Bureau
- Portuguese Trade & Tourism Office
- Reno Sparks Convention & Visitors Authority
- Rhode Island Economic Development
- Puerto Vallarta Convention & Visitors Bureau
- San Diego Convention & Visitors Bureau
- State of Vermont
- St. Kitts Tourism Authority
- St. Lucia Tourist Board
- St. Petersburg / Clearwater Area Convention & Visitors Bureau
- Tourist Office of Spain
- VisitBritian
- VisitScotland

CDMS has built relationships for the following destination organizations:
- America's Heartland
- Black Hills, Badlands & Lakes Association
- Kenya Tourist Board
- Mississippi River Country, U.S.A.
- Mississippi River Parkway Commission
- Minnesota Mississippi River Parkway Commission
- Patagonia Calling - www.patagoniacalling.com
- Stockholm Information Service
- Swedish Travel and Tourism Council

CDMS has provided consulting for the following organizations:
- Minnesota Office of Tourism
- Chemonics International
- US AID Project in Peru
- Missouri Division of Tourism
- University of Minnesota Tourism Center
- Washington State Tourism

8 Conclusion

Minnesota, as the selection for entrepreneurial leader in tourism services is predicated on their ability to turn theory into application. Relationship marketing is a largely undefined term. It may be used to convey a sense of familiarity between business and customer but it also means to create working relationships with those who act as intermediaries between a tourist service provider and their customer base. It relies on the theory of image formation processes first offered by Boulding (1956), brought firmly into the realm of tourism by Hunt (1973) and Gunn (1979) and further developed through the work of Gartner (1993). In its simplest forms relationship marketing uses travel specialists who are considered credible and with expertise when discussing a particular destination. Some of the most important and impressionable image formation agents come from those who have been to a place and write about it. Therefore using travel writers who have shown the ability to get their work published in recognized magazines is an important image formation agent. In a similar, but more direct manner, introducing travel operators to a new product for them may result in additional itineraries being developed and offered to their clients. The use of the media, in other ways, such as through the creation of documentaries also serves to develop, what are considered to be very credible image formation agents that also serve to reach large audiences.

Carlson Destination Marketing Services is a rarity in that it has studied the image formation process and made very practical applications of the theory. Their relationship marketing approach is outlined in the pages that follow together with examples of successful client programs. Their selection for this book was based on a assessment of travel service providers that have used novel approaches to creating customer demand. None were deemed to have been as forward thinking and as successful as Carlson Destination Marketing Services.

Frank M. Go

An Interpretation of Case Studies on Entrepreneurship and Innovation in Tourism

1   Introduction

This chapter seeks to interpret the cases featuring innovation in the context of selected entrepreneurs operating in a range of international tourism destinations. For purposes of analysis the cases were ordered in Table 1 according to four types of innovation (Tidd et al, 2005:10).

- *Product innovation* – changes in the things [products/services] which an organization offers;
- *Process innovation* – changes in the way they [products/services] are created and delivered;
- *Position innovation* – changes in the context in which products/services are introduced;
- *Paradigm innovation* – changes in the underlying mental models which frame what the organization does'.

In the present interpretation of multiple cases across divergent internal firm conditions, our examination found that country differences did not seem to play an inordinate role. The industry-specific environment can be relevant, however, for reasons Weiermaier explains in Chapter 2 "Tourism Development and Entrepreneurship". The destination life cycle appears to impact enterprises and to be most pressing and, also, most likely in forthcoming during the initiation/involvement stage and the consolidation/decline phase of innovative entrepreneurship. However, due to the very limited sample, it was inappropriate to conduct the present analysis from an "outside-inside" perspective. Therefore, our interpretation took an "inside-outside" perspective based on two main assumptions. First, that innovation is a learned behavior that can be applied by entrepreneurs in the tourism SME context. Second, that innovation determines the tourism SME growth potential, to a significant extent, under differing environmental conditions. Consequently, this chapter reveals recurring factors and sub-themes that seem to influence the innovation performance of entrepreneurs who were featured in the cases across both geographical and branch boundaries. The balanced score card (Kaplan & Norton, 1996) served to identify success factors (Table 2) that follow a hierarchy of vision and goals in order to achieve measurable performance results, as defined below.

Vision (i.e. human talent) is central to understanding entrepreneurial behaviour. But a focus on analysis that depends on a one-dimensional perspective typically fails to explain how entrepreneurs create and implement innovations.

1. The strategic aims (goals) refer to the end results an entrepreneur hopes to reach through his input, capacity or intention, operated by a human driven process.
2. The business score card provides a more "balanced view". All cases examine the innovation process in an entrepreneurial context, emphasizing different perspectives.
3. Critical success factors are those components of a management process, or any other human action, that must be carried out in the "right" manner for the achievement of goals;
4. Measures are indicators or key performance results used to determine differences in the outcome of a management process. Measures are used to describe the state or capacity of the system or network, the state of an entrepreneurial component, the state of its related social system or its components (output).

The role of innovation in enhancing competitiveness and justifying it for decision-makers, who emerge from ownership, key management roles and the political process has gained lately a new sense of urgency. For instance, when global warming, according to the OECD, threatens to reduce the number of Alpine winter-sport resorts from 599 to 500 banks refuse to provide loans to enterprises situated below 1,500 meters.

The question of "why entrepreneurs in the selected cases and tourism destinations pursue innovation", is easier posed than answered. An understanding of entrepreneurial motivation is needed to explain the origins and nature of the innovation process, not least because the sort of motive serves as a determining influence, firstly, upon the entrepreneur's choice of critical success factors; secondly, on the interpretation of a particular motivation selected largely determines and, therefore justifies, what sort of state policy should support it (see Chapter 1 by Keller).

Economic motives tend to be the most common justification for entrepreneurial innovation. Briefly stated, the popular argument is that innovation fuels the resilience of enterprises to adapt to changes in the business environment. When crisis confronts SMEs, survival depends on contingency planning supported by quick-response mechanisms to boost the "agility" which is needed to protect assets. Research into exemplary practice of entrepreneurially driven innovation is relevant for two main reasons. Firstly, cases such as the REKA bank demonstrate that it is possible "to double growth in core areas", despite factors that impede the promotion of tourism "productivity", particularly high production costs and competition based in low-wage countries (Keller, 2006). Secondly, the cases confirm that innovative firms such as CVC tour operator outperform their competition, despite adversary business conditions, including low consumer confidence born of political instability and double-digit inflation.

The political and governance justification is relevant due to the social character of the tourism network. For example, the REKA case underscores that the achievement of growth is "due neither to independent entrepreneurial innovators nor to a profit motive". Also, the Spa of Bochnia emphasises the entrepreneur's dependency of decision-making "at different levels of authority". Law and policymakers, through incentives and tax breaks shape the conditions for entrepreneurial activities including investment, construction and "modernisation of technical infrastructure and utilities." These observations compelled Keller (Chapter 1) to analyze, innovation from a government policy perspective and Weiermaier (Chapter 2) in the context of the destination life cycle.

Finally, it is important to enquire what "meaning and symbolic value" justifications might warrant stakeholders to support innovation diffusion, which depends on its adoption across branch, organizational, geographical and regulatory- and ethical boundaries. Undertaking an analysis which depends on social interaction by which a "constellation of stakeholders" and their objects of desire generate certain perceptions opens up a related line of enquiry into the significance of meaningful symbols. Methodologically, this implies a need to examine for example "product development and marketing in relation to an organizational philosophy" which is responsive to the community and cultural values (Peters et al, 2006).

2 Entrepreneurial Vision
2.1 Motivation

The role of the individual entrepreneur as a catalyst for innovation differs from firm-to-firm as confirmed by the vision of Bruce Poon of G.A.P. Adventures, Tanja Saarnio (TCF) Henk van Koeveringe (RP Care) and Joseph Kagerbauer Jr., of JOSKA. These cases demonstrate how successful tourism innovators are driven by their innate characteristics and personal qualities. For example, Tanja Saarnio of Touring Cars Finland (TCF) expresses same through her determination to conduct her business in an ethical manner whilst in pursuit of profit. Social value creation drives the REKA Bank to bring about "a symbiosis" between agriculture, social tourism and the Swiss para-hotel initiative. Finally, the entrepreneurial commitment "bubbling underneath" rises to the surface through the conscious lifestyle choice of the Scottish Ayrshire Food Network members and their pledge to contribute to environmental protection.

Their underlying mental model directs entrepreneurial energies not to gaining bureaucratic control but towards responsiveness to changes in demand and information management. In the process, it creates a sense of security allowing the abandonment of routines in favour of 'creative lunatics'.

2.2 Creativity and Risk-Averse Behaviour

The more unpredictable and uncertain the world is, the more entrepreneurs must rely on creativity to take advantage of "chaos" and "turbulence" in the business environment. Creativity is at the roots of value creation, but cannot be quantified. However, "creative imitation" and "outsourcing of innovative components and licenses" (Keller, 2006:12) can result in lower costs that can be passed on to customers resulting in a higher number of business transactions. For example, CVC tour operator "ten-month finance" policy without interest, refusal to incur "debts in dollar" to avoid the backlash of instable currency exchange and ability negotiate high-volume transactions with suppliers have led the number of passenger transactions to increase from 572,910 in 2002 to 1.47 million in 2005. The REKA cooperative society case profiles as to how the Swiss Travel Bank – banks are stereotyped as risk averse – applied a creative model of innovation enabling it to achieve a total of 1.265 rental transactions and simultaneously its quality of life goal by leveraging the domain of social tourism. The Touring Cars Finland case demonstrates how the cost of transferring motor-homes from Finland to Sweden and Norway was creatively reduced "by launching the Legoland package for Finnish customers."

2.3 Differentiation

One of the salient characteristics of the tourism sector is its binary competitive strategy of "internalization" and "collaboration". The former's high profile as expressed by major airlines, computer reservation systems, amusement parks and hotel chains has led many researchers to limit their enquiry to oligopolistic competition as "innovation driver". In contrast, monopolistic competition (Keller, 2006) is practiced by destination-embedded SME's such as Swarovski, JOSKA, CVC tour operator, and the Scottish Ayrshire Food Network which follow a unique selling proposition (Weiermair, 2006) to counter the stereotypical perception of tourism products. In particular, the Spa of Salt Mine Bochnia tries to position its product positively in the eyes of "well-heeled customers who can afford to pay higher prices." Hitherto, little thought has been given to examining methodologically the research issue whether the factor "differentiation" would be positively correlated with increased "barriers to innovation" (Keller, 2006:7).

3 Interpreting Cases across Different Stages of Market Development and Conditions

So what influences do different stages of economic development and divergent market conditions have on the innovation performance of entrepreneurs featured in the cases? As each region where the cases play faces its own distinctive issues and is subject to differences in the social, cultural and political systems it should be evident that the entrepreneurs featured across the cases face varying challenges that can be summarized broadly as follows.

In Europe the concern is one of managing a declining tourism sector with excess capacity in a stage of low demand, due, in part to high costs. This scenario has resulted in slow or no growth. In the emerging economies, including Brazil and Poland managing tourism growth under unstable conditions and weak infrastructure appears to prevail. In particular, the massive inflationary cycles since 1985, that reached a "high" of 1.000 per cent an "accomplishment" has been paralleled by only three other nations: Russia, Ukraine and Zaire cannot but affect negatively the innovation environment, including government policies and practices. Similarly, the Spa of Salt Mine Bochnia case reveals the serious impediments arising from the legacy "left by the centrally-planned economy", underdeveloped technical and transportation infrastructure, employment structures. It underscores the significance of the availability of financial-, human resources, and social values either as stimulants or impediments to innovation by tourism enterprises.

Whilst criticisms levelled at the innovation performance of SME's in the tourism sector may be justified to some extent, care should be taken to "tar them all with the same brush". The interpretation of cases reveals a more positive picture. It confirms the ability of selected entrepreneurs to apply innovation across their practice and outperform their competitors in spite of adverse conditions. For example, the REKA bank achieved doubled its growth; the Roompot, RP Care's parent company also almost doubled its sales results within two years; CVC Tour Operator became the largest tour operator of Brazil and the Spa of Salt Mine Bochnia took advantage of the privatization reforms in Poland.

However, as a consequence of deregulation and ICT competition has become global and raises the need for market conditions that enhance process – rather than product innovation (Weiermair, 2006:5). This implies that the cases examined and tourism enterprises in all countries for that matter, regardless of living standards, should benefit from governments removing barriers to competition, promoting fiscal responsibility, and ensuring "transparency of the law and a clear legal framework for property rights and regulatory oversights" (Global Entrepreneurship Monitor 2006; Babson College and the London Business School).

4 Interpreting Cases Across Critical Success Factors

In both the industrialized – and emerging economies an entrepreneur aims to reach his goals through his input, capacity, intention and talent - driven process. All cases examine the innovation process, lending greater emphasis on one of four different dimensions, namely the financial perspective, customer perspective, internal/business process perspective, learning and growth perspective (Table 2). In the framework of business score card an attempt was made to identify the most frequently cited factors that may explain, in part, how the entrepreneurs who are featured in the cases appear to achieve their goals.

4.1 Financial Perspective

Creativity: Creativity refers to the latent capability to problem solving; a process to take advantage of opportunity, move from ideas "to some physical reality" (Tidd et al, 2005: 92) which implies the need to invest and allocate resources. Astute investment is the root of success as witnessed by the creative financial schemes deployed by both REKA case and Touring Cars Finland (TCF) which enable the leveraging of assets and resources and pass on savings to clients and stakeholders. Reference to creative investments are also made in the case of G.A.P. Adventures (acquisition of a second expedition ship), Spa of Salt Mine Bochnia (private-public ownership). The Ayrshire Food Network chronicles how financial support is derived from various support agencies and "in kind" voluntary contributions from AFN-members.

4.2 Customer Orientation

Customer satisfaction: Customer satisfaction is a strong theme in five cases: Swarovski case, the JOSKA, The Spas of Salt Mine Bochnia case and CVC tour operator case; these emphasize the entrepreneur's ability to understand and act upon the needs of the client. For example, the REKA and, CVC Tour Operator case show how entrepreneurial sensitivity to the financial problems of low-budget households contributed to the popularization of holiday – consumption in both the Brazilian and Swiss case.

Quality Experience: It is particularly interesting to note that the innovative entrepreneurs featured in the cases recognize that the coordination of information and communication technologies is a prerequisite to the stimulation of creativity and collaboration. Both these factors must be "organized to fit successfully into the daily life of consumer and worker" (Go et al, 2001: 185). Consequently, the quality of the consumer-worker experience is affected by a collection of related events, rather than just a single event. In particular, the Swarovski case exemplifies how a sound integration of established functions enables the enterprise to connect to the consumers market in a totally different way, including staged events with new forms of marketing such as cooperative networks and co-branding.

New market development: The collaboration with a variety of societal stakeholders proved important for particularly JOSKA, Spa of Salt Mine Bochnia, and RP Care to develop new markets. For example, Spa of Salt Mine Bochnia, and RP Care did this through a process cross-fertilizing recreation and healthcare; whilst JOSKA developed a new process technique for sandblast engravings enabled the form to invent the World Cup crystal globe trophy for sports tournaments, resulting in business-to-business relations with major international brands and sport celebrities.

Internationalization: Internationalization is another strong theme recurring in six cases: the G.A.P. Adventures, REKA, Touring Cars Finland, Ayrshire Food Network, CVC Tour Operator and the Swarovski case. For example, the G.A.P. Adventures combined an export orientation combined with steady innovation anchored in destination image to attract a broadly geographically-based clientele.

4.3 Internal/Business Processes

Accessibility and Distribution: At least six cases identified the theme of access to a distribution system as essential. It comprises both retail outlets (JOSKA; Swarovski's 160 company-owned stores and 9,000 retail outlets; G.A.P. Adventures) and relations with intermediaries, including tour operators and travel agents (CVC Tour Operator) rental stations (Touring Cars Finland) and a network of 7,000 tourism enterprises who accept the REKA "traveller's cheques as a method of payment". Most cases referred to the importance of a website.

Cooperation and networking: The REKA case considered innovation issues in relation to the need for "support" in the form of "strategic partnerships". The need to acquire value-creating disciplines through "Industry and supporting organizations' in a climate of trust and mutual respect" was also underscored in the Ayrshire Food Network's emphasis on strong cluster linkages. The Touring Cars Finland, CVC Tour Operator cases provide further evidence that tourism networks with a common purpose play an important role both on the international level and local level (JOSKA and the RP Care).

Web-based efficiency and flexibility: Most cases refer to the increasing importance of information and communication technologies (ICTs) and websites in particular. Whilst tourism experiences are primarily enacted in the material space of a destination, the connectivity of places through a wide range of cyber-devices, affords greater process efficiency and flexibility. For example, the e-business portal of Ayrshire Food Network (AFN) facilitates marketing as well as firm alliances both business-to-business and business-to-consumer level and contributes to reducing cost, and by extension "increasing customer value, market share" (Weiermair, 2006: 4). It is linked to the Scottish Enterprise/Highlands and Islands Enterprise's Tourism Innovation Toolkit. Astutely REKA, Touring Cars Finland, JOSKA, RP Care, and CVC Tour Operator opted for a multiple-channel strategy. G.A.P. Adventures opted for a multiple-channel strategy, which combines physical and virtual marketing dimensions to serve the different customer profiles through an inter-active website, call centre and two concept stores in Toronto and Vancouver.

Membership and community: The recurring reference to the theme of "membership" indicates that "rents" are created through a joint process and "owned" by partnering firms. For example, Ayrshire Food Network (AFN) exemplifies a grass-roots initiative through the collective mobilisation of members' assets and resources on a complementary basis at all levels. Its organisation structure opens up new ways of working, innovation and business re-engineering for members; but also their thinking "relative to the heterogeneity of networks where a goal of sustainability in some cases may be inappropriate". Also, Touring Cars Finland and Swarovski apply the idea of "community" membership as a means of cultivating trustworthy relations with customers and partners alike (Go et al, 2001:187). The Swarovski case demonstrates how a corporate anniversary might serve as the impetus for institutionalizing the search of new ideas for products, culminating in its "collectors club". From a perspective of monopolistic competition trust as governance mechanism is most relevant. To promote membership and community particular features of embedded ties are: the mutual bridging of problems, accelerating decision-making processes, supporting inter-firm coordination and the promotion of learning (Go et al, 2001:191).

4.4   Learning and Growth

Knowledge transfer into competencies, products and experiences-based learning: REKA, Touring Cars Finland, Swarovski, JOSKA, CVC Tour Operator are cases that capture how entrepreneurs transformed an innovative environment into an experience-based learning process. In particular, the Touring Cars of Finland case, the REKA and the Scottish Ayrshire Food Network exemplify the changes in the underlying mental models which frame what the organization does. On a more down-to-earth level, CVC Tour Operator applies computer-based research to forecast tourists' preferences for the next season.

The JOSKA case and the RP Care case offer examples how "discontinuous" change leads to a greater dependency on knowledge and competencies and alterations in how products and services are created and delivered. Due to the blurring boundaries of branches innovation occurs increasingly in the "overlap" where two different knowledge domains meet; this is evident in four cases: the REKA, Touring Cars Finland, The Spas of Bochnia, and RP Care. For instance, the instalment of a dialysis centre in a RP holiday park meant that its managers had to learn about healthcare practice from local hospital professionals.

5   Concluding Remarks

The above ten themes were the predominant ones in terms of their breadth of applicability brought together in a range of cases. The featured entrepreneurs appear aware that future uncertainty raises both the need for innovation and an understanding of how to change.

What lessons do the cases hold? First, that the innovation "journey" takes time, energy, perseverance and a choice of innovation type (products, process, position and paradigm). Second, that creativity may be viewed as a lever to harness distributed ideas to turn resource scarcity into opportunity through a change in service process design and by allocating resources in a different way, where appropriate. Third, that success resides in an attitude of leading change rather than denying it; outsourcing to reduce costs and jointly-create "novel" products.

The cases underscore that change is an imperative for growth. But conventional wisdom has it, that everyone wants progress but no one wants change. So what do our observations imply for the entrepreneurial innovation journey, including their rate of diffusion, consequences for the structure, competitive forces and contribution to the financial performance of the tourism sector?

Firstly, a knowledge-based economy demands insight into the distribution of innovation capability, particularly with regard to strategy, organization, linkages, learning and processes that distinguish successful- from unsuccessful entrepreneurs. Secondly, as the capacity to innovate is rooted in a "high-order integration capability", i.e. managing multiple capabilities, which causes a governance dilemma of unlearning assumptions that underlie traditional business practices and learning new capabilities for the future. It calls for an organizational context and agenda to support entrepreneurs in this regard (IEN Network). Finally, the knowledge and competences gathered through the network can serve as both a guide and resource to support those entrepreneurs, who are presently unaware either what or how to improve their innovation performance and competitiveness.

References

Go, F.M., & Appelman, J. (2001), Achieving global competitiveness in SMEs by building trust in interfirm alliances, in: Tourism in the Age of Globalisation, S. Wahab & C. Cooper, London: Routledge, pp. 183–197.

Keller, Peter (2006), Innovation and tourism policy, Paper presented at the 77th Session of the OECD Tourism Committee, Rome, 22 June, Paris OECD.

Peters, M., Weiermair, K, Katawandee, P, (2006), Strategic brand management of tourism destinations: Creating emotions and meaningful intangibles, in: Marketing Efficiency in Tourism Coping with Volatile Demand, Keller, Peter & T. Bieger (eds.), pp. 65–79.

Tidd, J., Bessant, J., & Pavitt, K (2005), Managing Innovation Integrating technological, market and organizational change, Chicester: Wiley.

Weiermair, Klaus (2004), Product Improvement or Innovation: What is the key to success in Tourism, Paper presented at the 77th Session of the OECD Tourism Committee, Rome, 22 June, Paris: OECD.

Appendix

Authors	Types of Innovation	Sub-theme
1.	**Product Innovation – Changes in Things Offered**	
1.1 Pechlaner, Harald & Fischer, Elisabeth	Investigates how the hybridization of different businesses resulted in leadership, globally in glass trophy manufacturing and locally in tourism	Entrepreneurial competencies
1.2 Weiermair, Klaus & Kronenberg, Christopher	Chronicles the transformation of crystal products into cultural tourism experience	Experience-based organizational platform
2.	**Process Innovation: Changes in the way of creation and delivery**	
2.1 Morrison, A & Lynch, Paul	Reviews a model for translating a re-generation vision into a grass roots process initiative involving the food chain in a sustainable manner	Community entrepreneurship
2.2 Brooker, Ed & Go, Frank	Examines how a blending of healthcare and recreation affords RP Care to leverage disruptive innovation opportunities	Modular business model
2.3 Fischer, Eileen and Markarem, Samir	Profiles an adventure eco-tour venture model that links niche-marketing and imagery of the unspoiled wilderness with company expertise and options	Export orientation and product innovation
3.	**Position Innovation: Changes in the Context**	
3.1 Golembski, Grzegorz & Olszewski, Marcin	Identifies both impediments and stimulants in the political and economic environment in the Polish context	Tourism product enhancement and differentiation
3.2 Trigo, L.G.G	Argues that a 'powerful' management team can achieve market leadership in spite of tourism risks and extreme turbulent political and economic conditions	Crisis management in an emerging market
3.3 Carlson Destination Marketing	Investigates an approach that leverages market -, media, regional intelligence and resources in a targeted destination relationship strategy	Channel network partnership

Services		
4.	**Paradigm Innovation: Changes in the Underlying Mental Mode**	
4.1 Keller, Peter	Profiles a creative model of innovation designed to increase prosperity and improve the quality of life	Social tourism
4.2 Komppu-la, Raija	Proposes that high-order integration capability is a prerequisite for innovation capacity	Business idea and core values

Table 1: Innovation Typology for Case Analysis

Strategic Aims	Balanced Scorecard Perspective	Selected Examples
	Critical Success Factors	
Financial Perspective	Creativity/ culture of innovation	Leveraging assets and resources; VAT deductions; amortization benefits
Customer orientation Perspective	Customer satisfaction	(fair prices)
	Quality Experience	Quality 1.2; 2.1; 2.2; Experiences (Emotionalizing artifacts/locations)
	New market development	Taking advantage of opportunity1.2; 2.4; 3.1
	Internationalization	
	Occupancy rates (e.g. overnight stays)	REKA; Roompot
Internal/ Business Processes Perspective	Accessibility and Distribution	website; e-business portal; Distribution system (retail outlets; geographic reach)
	Cooperation and networking	collaboration; clustering Common purpose; Team-play; Support
	Efficiency and flexibility	
	Membership and community	community projects
Learning and Growth Perspective	Transfer knowledge into competencies/new products	
	Professionalism	marketing; ethics; preservation; Authenticity 1.1; 1.2; 2.4

Key Performance Results	Measures	Selected Examples
	Growth in turnover	
	Number of tourist arrivals; passengers	the number of passengers carried by CVC tour operator rose from 572,910 in 2002 to 1,47 million in 2005;
	Awards and recognitions	the G.A.P. Adventures carries 40,000 passengers annually was ranked for five consecutive years as one 'of the 50 fastest growing companies in Canada';
	Net Financial Results	Roompot (RPCare) doubled its net financial results from EUR 68.4 million in 2002 to EUR 118.4 million in 2004

Table 2: Balanced Scorecard Perspectives to Improve Tourism SME Performance